KARATEDO KATA MODEL

新装版

空手道形教範

指定形

セーパイ
SEIPAI

セイエンチン
SEIENCHIN

サイファ
SAIFA

バッサイ(大)
BASSAI(DAI)

for TEACHING

財団法人　全日本空手道連盟：編
Japan Karatedo Federation

ジオン
JION

セイシャン
SEISHAN

観空(大)
KANKU(DAI)

チントウ
CHINTO

SHITEIGATA

ベースボール・マガジン社

セーパイ
SEIPAI

サイファ
SAIFA

ジオン
JION

観空（大）
KANKU(DAI)

セイエンチン
SEIENCHIN

バッサイ(大)
BASSAI(DAI)

セイシャン
SEISHAN

チントウ
CHINTO

序文

財団法人　全日本空手道連盟
会長　笹川　堯

　人が生きていくためには、健康な身体と社会生活に必要な知識と、そして誰もがお互い敵としない友愛の心いわゆる"和を以て尊し"の精神がなければならず、このことが一つ欠けても人類の繁栄はありません。

　空手道は本来、外敵から己を守り生きていくために発達した武術でありましたが、現代では、健康な身体に教養と、社会に協調する精神を身につけるために、有効な教育の手段であることが認識されて世界中に普及されております。今後も空手道が現代に生きる武道として、生涯を通じて全世界の人々に愛されるためには、武道の技と心を基盤としたスポーツとして味わいのあるものにしていかなければならないと考えております。

　空手道を立派な人を育てるために広く普及させるためには、強い情熱と理念をもった指導者の育成が必要ですが、そのために空手道の正しい伝統的技術の継承と科学的論理を基盤とする指導書の作成が最も必要とされます。今回の19年振りに新たに修正を加えて発行される、『空手道形教範』は大変意義深いものがあります。

　これからも一人でも多くの人に空手道を親しんでいただきたいと思い、生涯にわたって続ける武道スポーツとして親しまれるように、連盟としても一層の努力をしていきたいと思います。

Preface

President Japan Karatedo Federation
Takashi Sasagawa

In order to lead a useful life one needs to maintain a healthy body and knowledge of the spirit of " WA" or perfect harmonious relations among friends without hostility. One can not extend human prosperity without one of these factors.

Originally, Karatedo had developed as a martial art to protect oneself from enemies. However, it has come to be known as an effective educational means to cultivate culture for healthy body and motivate high spirit of cooperation in society.

To have a worldwide support as a martial art in the modern world ,Karatedo must develop to be an enjoyable sport based on skillful technique and strong mind.

In order to spread the wisdom of Karatedo widely as a means to raise healthy adults it is very important to have leading instructors who can display a strong enthusiasm and philosophy for which an appropriate text book must be prepared. It is thus significant that a newly revised edition of text book "KARATEDO KATA KYOHAN" will be published shortly, 19 years after the original release of the book.

I hope that Japan Karatedo Federation will do its best to invite as many friends as possible who are interested in Karatedo and who will continue to enjoy Budo Sport in their lives.

はじめに

財団法人　全日本空手道連盟
副会長／専務理事　蓮見圭一

　人格の完成を目指し、その目的に到達する過程と道理を「道」とされ、華道、茶道、武道……あらゆる「道」は、まず形から入る。形から入ることにより心を得るといわれています。

　空手道においても、心と肉体の調和を学ぶために考案されたものが形であります。形の繰り返しの修練により、どんな技の変化にも対応できる俊敏にして強靭な身体と、礼節を重んじた謙虚な態度となにものにも臆さない精神を養うことで、形の修行が重視されています。

　形に織り込まれた全ての技を、その意味を理解し正確に演じ、無駄な技を省くことで正しさと素朴さを、繰り返すことで忍耐と勤勉を、精神を超越し、さらにもう一歩深く求めることにより、その完成に近づく姿は心身ともに健康で優雅にさえ見えるものでありましょう。

　空手道の形は、伝統的に継承される流派の特徴をもった形が数多く存在し、同じ名称の形でも流派の系統により少しづつ違うので、(財)全日本空手道連盟では、会派団体である四大流派の中から代表的なおのおの二つの形を選出し、8つの形を指定形と制定しました。

　今回の出版は、1982年11月に制定発行した『空手道指定型』に、伝統的技術論理に基づいた見直しと分解と解説を加えて発行いたしました。最初に発行された本書は、日本国内はもとより世界の空手道の発展普及に計り知れない大きな役割を果たしました。今更ながら、当時の関係者の決断とその努力に心からなる感謝と敬意を表します。

　今回の発行に当り、(財)全日本空手道連盟の構成団体である会派のご理解とご協力に感謝いたします。そして、本書『空手道形教範』の発行がさらなる空手道の発展につながることを念じ、発行にあたってのご挨拶といたします。

Introduction

Vice President / Chief Director Japan Karatedo Federation
Keiichi Hasumi

The process and reason for developing the human character is to understand "do" or "profound truth", All traditional arts in Japan (the"do"arts) Kado(flower arrangement), Sado(tea ceremony) and Budo(martial art) begin with KATA. It is said that through concentrating on the practice of KATA, the profound essence of truth in the art will be mastered.

In Karatedo, KATA is designed to action harmony of heart with body. By repeated training of KATA one can build up an agile and strong body, a modest and courteous attitude, and a fearless spirit to overcome any threat and cope with any attack.

Various kinds of WAZA or techniques incorporated in KATA are studied in order to acquire patience and diligence by repeating the training of KATA based on an understanding of the deep meaning of the art in its simplicity while avoiding useless actions. A sincere effort to understand the essence of truth through devotion to training will develop an attractive and healthy attitude.

Traditionally, there are many types of KATA in Karatedo and thus one finds the word KATA incorporated in the same name of many Karate schools. Despite this there are many differences among the various schools.

The Japan Karatedo Federation, therefore, selected two representative types of KATA from each of the four major schools and designated a total of eight Kata as SHITEIGATA.

This book is a revised edition of "Karatedo Shiteigata" published in November, 1982. In this new edition there are added revisions, analysis and comments based on the traditional theories and techniques.

The first edition of this book greatly contributed to the development of Karatedo not only in Japan but all over the world. On this occasion I would like to extend my heartfelt respect and gratitude to all those involved in the publication of this book.

Thank you again to the members of Japan Karatedo Federation for their invaluable cooperation to make this publication possible. I hope this new book will contribute to the further development of Karatedo.

目次　　　　　　　　　　　　　　CONTENTS

序　文　　　笹川　堯
はじめに　　蓮見　圭一

セーパイ篇　　　SEIPAI ——————— 7

サイファ篇　　　SAIFA ——————— 31

ジオン篇　　　JION ——————— 47

観空(大)篇　　　KANKU(DAI) ——————— 75

セイエンチン篇　　　SEIENCHIN ——— 113

バッサイ(大)篇　　　BASSAI(DAI) — 137

セイシャン篇　　　SEISHAN ——————— 165

チントウ篇　　　CHINTO ——————— 189

セーパイ篇

〔特徴〕

セーパイは逆技・投げ技など接近戦での護身術として効果的な技が多い。特に巧妙な円の動きが特徴である。攻防技が一連になっていて緩急の動作をリズミカルにすることが求められる。

SEIPAI has plenty of effective techniques for self-defense in Sekkin-Sen such as reversal and throwing techniques. A special characteristic of SEIPAI is the use of circular movements in it techniques. It is necessary that defensive and offensive techniques flow rhythmically from one to the other.

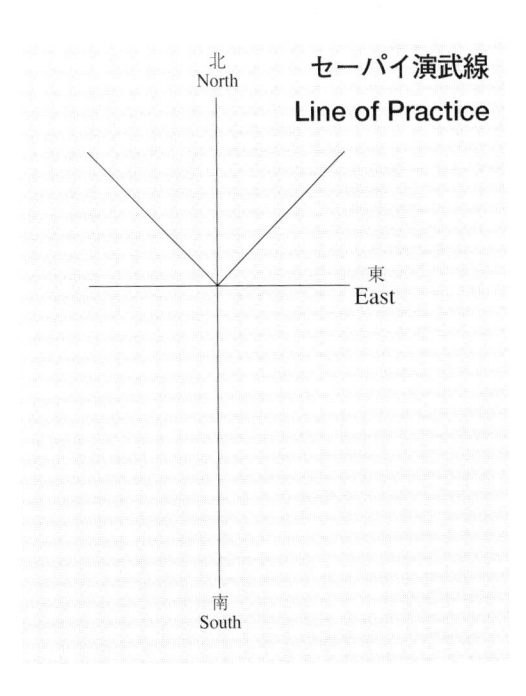

セーパイ演武線
Line of Practice

北 North
東 East
南 South

SEIPAI

直立（用意） 1挙動

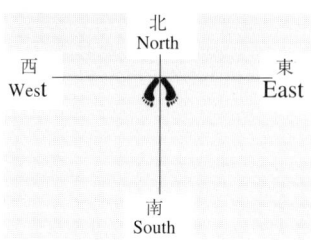

足の動作●結び立ち。
立ち方●結び立ち。
手の動作●両手は開いて大腿部両側に付けて伸ばす。

Remarks
1:Feet
2:Stance
3:Hands
4:Point to see

1:Musubidachi
2:Musubidachi
3:Open both hands and move stretched arms.

足の動作●結び立ち。
立ち方●結び立ち。
手の動作●両手を開き金的の前に構える（左手前、右手後ろ）。

留意点●呼吸は「短呑」

着眼点●南（正面やや高め）

1:Musubidachi
2:Musubidachi
3:Open both hands, place them in front of Kinteki (groin), with left hand on top.
4:South (slightly upward)

Point:Breath Tan-don (inhale briefly)

足の動作●両爪先を軸に平行立ちとなる。
立ち方●平行立ち。
手の動作●両手を握りながら両体側へ手の甲を外側に構える。

留意点●呼吸は「長吐」。丹田を中心に全身に力を入れる。

着眼点●南

1:Pivoting on the toes, move heels outward until parallel.
2:Heikodachi
3:Clenching the fists, move them to the sides, with the back of the hand facing outwards.
4:South

Point:Exhale deeply while tensing the body, concentrating the whole strength in the Tanden(abdomen).

セーパイ

2 挙動

④

【④を東から見る】
④ seen from east.

⑤

⑥

足の動作●左足を北の方向に引いて右四股立ちとなる。
立ち方●四股立ち。
手の動作●左開掌。指先を上に顔の前で半円を描きながら水月の前で構える。並行して右縦貫手は左腕の内側から上より半円を描くように南方向に腕をまっすぐ伸ばす。肘に余裕を持たせる。
留意点●四股立ち。腰が高く両膝が内にしぼんでしまわないようにする。

着眼点●南

1: Pull left foot back toward north, then, Right-Shikodachi.
2: Shikodachi
3: With fingers pointing upward left Kaisho, trace a small semi-circle from the side, towards the front of the face, ending in front of the abdomen. At the same time, from the inside of the left arm, trace a bigger semi-circle with the right arm, stretching to the front. Relax both elbows.
4: South
Point: Shikodachi:
Do not stand up with high hip position and avoid inward twisting the knees.

足の動作●左足を南方向に踏み出す。
立ち方●左足前平行立ち（締めは三戦）。
手の動作●左手を右手の下に添えて両手を握り合わせる（右手の位置で右手上、左手下の合掌握り）。

着眼点●南

1: Step left foot forward to south.
2: Step forward left foot. Heikodachi. Sanchinsime (left foot in front)
3: Grip both palms, with left hand underneath right hand (Gassho Nigiri).
4: South

挙動の分解2　Seipai Kumite in detail

①

挙動の分解3　Seipai Kumite in detail

②

【❽を東から見る】

❽ seen from east.

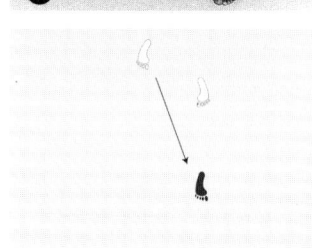

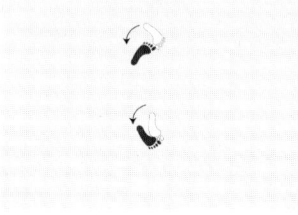

足の動作●右足を南方向に１歩踏み出す。
立ち方●左足前平行立ち。
手の動作●合掌に握ったまま、その位置で、両手首を反らしながらひねり込む（左手上、右手下の合掌握り）。

留意点●両手首のひねり込みが終ってから踏み出さない様注意する。

着眼点●南

1: Take right foot one step foward to south.
2: Heikodachi (left foot in front)
3: Gripping palms (Gassho) in the same position, stretch both wrists backward, while twisting wrists clockwise (left hand on top).
4: South

Point: Avoid moving forward after completion of the arm movement.

挙動の分解 3　Seipai Kumite in detail

セーパイ

3 挙動

⑩

足の動作●両爪先の方向を変え、四股立ちとなる。
立ち方●四股立ち。
手の動作●合掌に握ったまま右肘を肩の高さに跳ねあげる。

着眼点●南（体は東）

1: Change direction of toes, then, Shikodachi
2: Shikodachi
3: Gripping palms (Gassho) pull right elbow quickly up to shoulder height.
4: South (body faces east)

4 挙動

⑪

【⑪を西から見る】
⑪ seen from west.

⑫

足の動作●左足を南方方向に出し、左足前、後屈立ちとなる。
立ち方●後屈立ち。
手の動作●左開掌にて腕を体の線に平行になるように伸ばし、下段掌低当て、右肘は肩より高くあげ、腕、掌を伸ばし、体の線に平行になるように下に向ける。
留意点●左手は右手の内側より円を描きながら下段掌低当てをする。

着眼点●南（体は西）

1: Step left foot forward to south.
2: Kokutsudachi (left foot in front)
3: Left hand Kaisho, stretch left arm parallel to the side, executing Gedan-Shoteiate. Pull right elbow higher than shoulder height, with arm and palm facing downward, stretch parallel to center line of the body.
4: South (body faces west)

Point: Left hand Gedan-Shoteiate after making an arc from inside of right hand.

挙動の分解4
Seipai Kumite in detail

⑤

⓭

⓮

【⓭を西から見る】

⓭ seen from west.

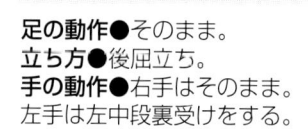

⓯

足の動作●そのまま。
立ち方●後屈立ち。
手の動作●右手はそのまま。
左手は左中段裏受けをする。

着眼点●南（体は西）

1: Same as in ⓫.
2: Kokutsudachi
3: Right hand same as in ⓫. Left hand executes Chudan Urauke
4: South (body faces west)

足の動作●両足を軸に南方向に半前屈になるよう、体の向きを変える。
立ち方●左半前屈立ち。
手の動作●右上段手刀外回し打ち。左開掌は掌を前向に左脇に構える。
留意点●左手首がまっすぐにならない様にする（手首で相手攻撃を押える）。

着眼点●南

1: Pivoting on both balls of the feet, shift body direction toward south.
2: Left-Half-Zenkutsudachi
3: Jyodan side blow attack with right Shuto. Left hand Kaisho, with palm facing forward, hold it under left armpit.
4: South
Point: Wrist must not straighten without bending (press down opponent's attack with wrist).

拳動の分解5　Seipai Kumite in detail

⑥　⑦　⑧

12

セーパイ

⑯ ⑰ ⑱

【⑰を西から見る】
⑰ seen from west.

足の動作●右中段前蹴り。
立ち方●片足立ち。
手の動作●⑮のまま。

留意点●左手が脇から離れない様注意。

着眼点●南

1:Right Chudan-Maegeri
2:Standing on left foot.
3:Same as in ⑮.
4:South

Point: Don't separate left hand from the body.

足の動作●右足を北方向に引き、四股立ちとなる。
立ち方●四股立ち。
手の動作●左中段回し肘当て。右拳は脇に引く。

留意点●肘が前方に出すぎない様注意。

着眼点●南（体は西）

1:Pull down right foot toward north,then,Shikodachi.
2:Shikodachi
3:Left Chudan-Mawashi-Hijiate. Right fist remains the same.
4:South (body faces west)
Point: Do not overextend left elbow.

▶セーパイ篇 13

5 挙動

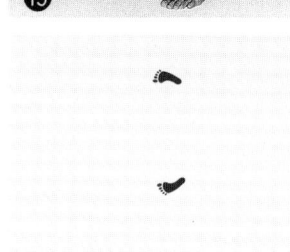

⑲

⑳ 【⑲を西から見る】
⑲ seen from west

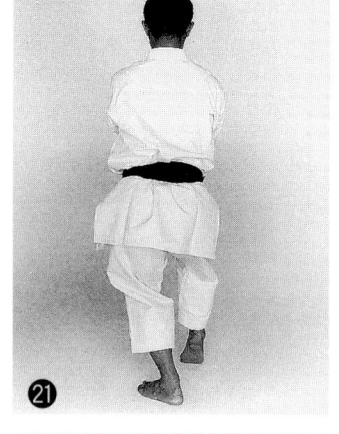

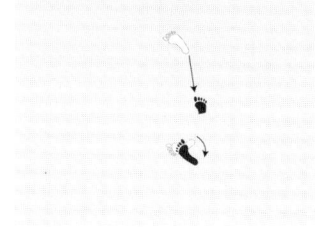

㉑

㉒ 【㉑を北から見る】
㉑ seen from north

足の動作●⑰のまま。
立ち方●四股立ち。
手の動作●左上段裏拳打ち。
右拳は脇に引いたまま。

着眼点●南（体の西）

足の動作●左足を軸に体を90°回転、北方向を向き、右足を寄せて右足前猫足立ちとなる。
立ち方●右猫足立ち。
手の動作●右拳は下段受け、左拳は甲を上に右肘の下に構える。

着眼点●北

1:Same as in ⑰.
2:Shikodachi
3:Left-Jyodan-Uraken-Uchi.
　Right fist remains the same.
4:South (body faces west)

1:Pivoting on left foot. turn body 90 degree toward north and pull right foot into Right-Nekoashidachi
2:Nekoashidachi (right foot in front)
3:Right-Gedan-Uke. Hold right fist under right elbow with back of hand facing upward.
4:North

14

セーパイ

6 挙動

㉓

㉔ 【㉓を北から見る】
㉓ seen from north

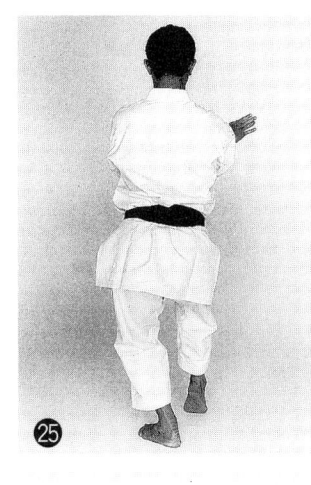

㉕

㉖ 【㉕を北から見る】
㉕ seen from north

足の動作●㉑のまま。
立ち方●右猫足立ち。
手の動作●右拳は右中段横受けをし、拳を返しながら甲を上に開掌にして掛け受けをする。左拳はそのまま。

着眼点●北

1:Same as in ㉑.
2:Nekoashidachi (right foot in front)
3:Chudan-Yokouke with right fist. Perform Kakeuke by twisting hands inward from Kaisho. Left fist remains same.
4:North

挙動の分解6　　Seipai Kumite in detail

⑩　　⑪　　⑫

▶セーパイ篇　15

【㉗から㉘の途中を北西から見る】
㉗ to ㉘ seen from north west

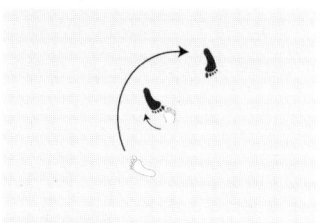

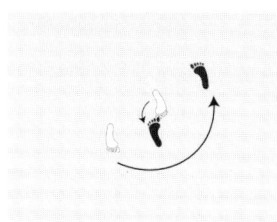

足の動作●右足を軸に体を180°回転、南方向に右足前三戦立ちとなる。
立ち方●右三戦立ち。
手の動作●右開掌は握りながら左斜め下に締め込む。左拳は顔の前辺より半円を描くように下に回し、胸の前で右拳と交差したのち、左脇にしめる（相手の右肘関節を極める）。
留意点●左手首が体の前に出ない様脇をしめる。

着眼点●南

1:Pivoting on right foot, turn body 180 degree toward south then, Sanchindachi with right foot in front.
2:Sanchindachi (right foot in front)
3:While moving left fist up, then bringing it, downward in semi-circular motion, clench right hand. Then shoving downward diagonally to the left side. Crossing with right fist in front of chest, stopping under left side body. (joint of opponent's right elbow is captured)
4:South

Point: Squeeze left side body with keeping left wrist does not come in front of body.

挙動の分解7　Seipai Kumite in detail

16

7 挙動

セーパイ

㉛

㉜ 【㉛を北西から見る】
㉛ seen from northwest.

㉝ 【㉝を北西から見る】
㉞ ㉝ seen from northwest.

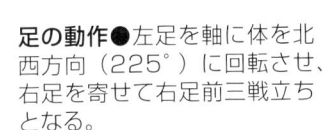

足の動作●左足を軸に体を北西方向（225°）に回転させ、右足を寄せて右足前三戦立ちとなる。
立ち方●右三戦立ち。
手の動作●左拳は開掌にして顔面前より円を描きながら掌を上前方にして左脇に構える。右拳は開掌にして腕を下に伸ばし、右掌にて下より上にはねあげる（弾指打ち）。
留意点●弾指打ち、手首のスナップを効かすようにする。

着眼点●北西

足の動作●左足より寄り足にて北西へ前進して三戦立ちとなる。
立ち方●三戦立ち。
手の動作●左開掌を右肩前より回して掌底にて下段押さえ受け。右掌底は右下より左肩の方へ押し上げる（支え上げ受け）。

着眼点●北西

1: Slide forward holding left Sanchindachi (left foot at first)
2: Sanchindachi. (left foot in front)
3: Swing left hand from front of right shoulder and, conclude movement with Gedan-Osaeuke by Shotei (palmheel). Push up right Shotei toward left shoulder.
4: Northwest

1: Pivoting on left foot, turn body 225 degree toward northwest, then, into Right-Sanchindachi
2: Sanchindachi (right foot in front)
3: Left fist to Kaisho, after drawing a circle in front of the face, hold it under left armpit, with palm facing up forward. Right fist to Kaisho, extend arm downward, then, snap upward with right palm (attack with fingers).
4: Northwest

Point: Attack with fingers. Use right wrist snap effectively.

挙動の分解 7　Seipai Kumite in detail

⑭

▶ セーパイ篇　17

8 挙動

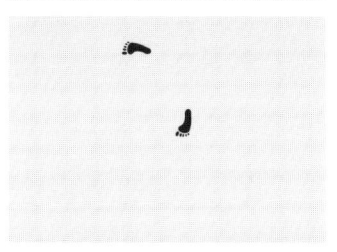

足の動作●右足を北西方向に進め、四股立ちとなる。
立ち方●四股立ち。
手の動作●両掌を向かい合わせて水月部前に構える（左手下、右手上、天地の構え）。

留意点●四股立ちをしてから両掌を構えない。

着眼点●北西（体は南西）

足の動作●右足で足払いをする。
立ち方●
手の動作●両掌を握りながら引きつける。両拳は乳の辺り。

留意点●肘が外へ出ないよう気を付ける。

着眼点●北西→南西

足の動作●右足を元の位置にもどし、腰を落とし、深い四股立ちとなる。
立ち方●四股立ち。
手の動作●両掌が外向きになるように両正拳で下突き。

留意点●気合を入れる。腰は出来るだけ低くする。

着眼点●南西

1: Step right foot forward to north west into Shikodachi.
2: Shikodachi
3: Facing both palms each other, hold them in front of abdomen (right hand above, left hand below)
4: Northwest (body faces southwest)

Point: Don't face both palms after Shikodachi.

1: Ashibarai with right foot.
2:
3: Clenching both palms pull both elbow toward body until fists are about the level of breast.
4: Northwest→Southwest

Point: Keep elbows close to the side of the body so as not it comes outside.

1: Return right foot to the original position, then, drop hips low.
2: Deep Shikodachi
3: With back of the hands facing outside, execute hands Gedan-Seikentsuki with both hands.
4: Southwest

Point: Perform with shout of Kiai "Ei!" Drop hips as low as possible.

9 挙動

㊳

㊴

㊵

【㊴を北東から見る】

㊴ seen from northwest

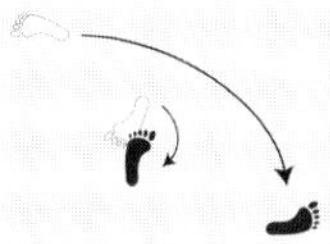

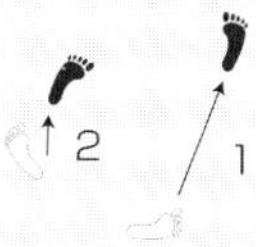

足の動作●左足を軸に右足を南東（180゜）方向に引き、四股立ちとなる。
立ち方●四股立ち。
手の動作●左払い受け。右拳は右脇に構える。

着眼点●北西（体は北東）

1:Pivoting on left foot, swing right foot 180 degree toward southeast.
2:Shikodachi
3:Left-Gedan-Uke Hold right fist under right armpit.
4:Northwest (body faces northeast)

足の動作●右足より寄り足にて北東へ前進して三戦立ちとなる。
立ち方●右三戦立ち。
手の動作●右開掌を左肩前より回して掌底にて下段押え受け。左掌底は左下より右肩の方へ押し上げる（支え上げ受け）。

着眼点●北東

1:Step forward with drag (right foot first) toward northeast to be Sanchindachi
2:Sanchindachi (right foot in front)
3:Swing right hand Kaisho in circular motion from front of left shoulder and, conclude movement with Gedan-Osaeuke by Shotei. Push up left Shotei from below left side toward direction of right shoulder (Sasae-ageuke).
4:North Sasae-ageuke east

挙動の分解 8　Seipai Kumite in detail

⑮

⑯

⑰

⑱

10挙動

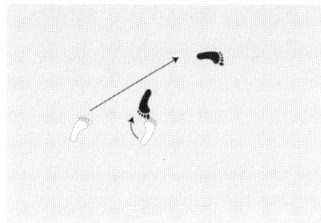

㊶ ㊷ ㊸

足の動作●左足を北東方向に進め、四股立ちとなる。
立ち方●四股立ち。
手の動作●両掌を向かい合わせて水月部前に構える（左手上、右手下）。天地の構え。

着眼点●北東（体は南東）

足の動作●左足で足払いをする。
立ち方●左払い足。
手の動作●両掌は握りながら、引きつける。両拳は乳の辺り。

着眼点●北東→南東

足の動作●左足を元の位置にもどし、腰を落とし、深い四股立ちとなる。
立ち方●四股立ち。
手の動作●両拳が外向きになるように両正拳で下突き。

留意点●気合を入れる。

着眼点●南東

1: Step left foot forward to northeast.
2: Shikodachi
3: Facing both palms each other, hold them in front of abdomen (left hand above, right hand below).
4: Northeast(body faces southeast)

1: Ashibarai with left foot.
2: Stand on right foot.
3: Clenching both palms, pull both elbows until fists are about breast level.
4: Northeast→Southeast

1: Return left foot to original position, then, drop hips low.
2: Deep Shikodachi
3: With back fists facing outside, execute Gedantsuki with both Seiken
4: Southeast

Point: Perform with shout of Kiai "Ei!"

11挙動　　　　　　　　　　　　　　　　セーパイ
　　　　　　　　　　　　　　　　　　　12挙動

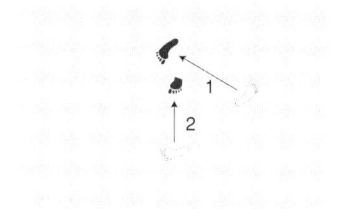

足の動作●右足を軸に左足を南西（180°）方向に引き、四股立ちとなる。
立ち方●四股立ち。
手の動作●右下段払い受け。左拳は左脇に構える。

着眼点●北東（体は北西）

1: Pivoting on right foot, swing left foot 180 degree toward southwest.
2: Shikodachi
3: Right Gedan-Haraiuke. Hold left fist under left armpit.
4: Northeast (body faces northwest)

足の動作●右足を左足の北方向に1歩出し、体を南方向（135°）に回転させ、半身となり左足を引きつけ、左前猫足立ちとなる。
立ち方●左猫足立ち。

着眼点●南

手の動作●左中段横受け。右拳は上段振り打ちをする（右拳は額の前で止める）。
留意点●体の向きはやや半身になる。

着眼点●南

挙動の分解12　Seipai Kumite in detail

1: Take right foot one step toward north of left foot, turn body 135 degree toward south, then, pull back left foot together to stand Nekoashidachi.
2: Nekoashidachi (left foot in front)
3: Left-Chudan-Yokouke. Jyodan-Furiuchi with right fist (stop right fist in front of the forehead).
4: South
Point: The direction of the body faces slightly Hanmi.

13挙動

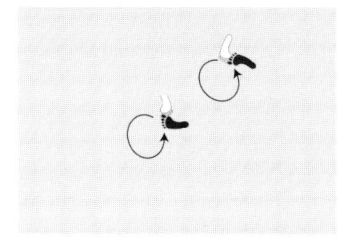

【㊾を西から見る】
㊾ seen from west

足の動作●右足を左足の南方向に進め、右弁足立ちとなる。
立ち方●弁足立ち。
手の動作●右中段横受け。左拳は上段振り打ちをする（左拳は額の前で止める）。

着眼点●南

1: Step right foot forward to south of left foot to cross feet to stand Bensokudachi.
2: Bensokudachi
3: Right-Chudan-Yokouke. Jyodan-Furiuchi with right fist (stop left fist in front of forehead).
4: South

足の動作●体を左へ270°回転させ、西向き三戦立ちとなる。
立ち方●左三戦立ち。
手の動作●左中段掛け受け。右は開掌で甲を上に右脇に構える。

留意点●転身は素早く掛け受け、肘をしめる。

着眼点●西

1: Turn body 270 degree toward left, facing west to stand Sanchindachi.
2: Sanchindachi (left foot in front)
3: Left-Chudan-Kakeuke. Right hand to Kaisho, with back of hand facing upward, hold it under right armpit.
4: West

Point: Swift in body turn and Kakeuke (hook block). Hold elbow under right armpit.

挙動の分解13〜15　Seipai Kumite in detail

セーパイ

㊾ 【㋑を北から見る】
㋑ seen from north

㊿ 【㋒を北から見る】
㋒ seen from north

足の動作●体をひねり右足前半後屈立ちとなる。
立ち方●半後屈立ち。
手の動作●左半打拳にて下段打ち。右開掌は握りながら右脇に構える。
下段打ちから連続して上段裏拳打ちをする。
両足の向きを変えるのと腰のひねり、右膝を曲げるのを一気にすることで切れのある方向転換が出来る。

着眼点●西（体は北）

1: Twist body to be Half-Kokutsudachi (right foot in front).
2: Half-Kokutsudachi
3: While doing Gedan-Uchi with Left-Half-Daken. Clench right hand Kaisho, hold it under right armpit, then Jodan Uraken-Uchi. Simultaneously twist both feet clockwise then, twisting hips and bending right knee sharp turn are possible.
4: West (body faces north)

足の動作●㋑のまま。
立ち方●半後屈立ち。
手の動作●左上段裏拳打ち。
体、右拳はそのまま。

着眼点●西（体は北）

1: Same as in ㋑.
2: Half-Kokutsudachi
3: Left-Jyodan-Uraken-Uchi. Body and right fist remain the same.
4: West (body faces north)

挙動の分解7　Seipai Kumite in detail

㉑　㉒　㉓　㉔

▶セーパイ篇　23

14挙動

⑤

⑥

足の動作●体を西の方向に捻り、左足前三戦立ちにもどる。
立ち方●左三戦立ち。
手の動作●右中段横受け。左拳は左脇に構える。

着眼点●西

1: Twist body toward west, returning to Sanchindachi.
2: Sanchindachi (left foot in front)
3: Right-Chudan-Yokouke. Hold left fist under left armpit.
4: West

足の動作●右中段前蹴り。
立ち方●片足立ち。
手の動作●手の構えは㊺のまま。

着眼点●西

1: Right-Chudan-Maegeri
2: Stand on left foot.
3: Same as in ㊺.
4: West

15挙動

⑤⑦

⑤⑧

【㊼を北から見る】
㊼ seen from north

足の動作●右足を東の方向に引き、四股立ちとなる。
立ち方●四股立ち。
手の動作●左中段裏突き（逆拳）右手は開掌、指先を上に水月の前に構える（押え受け）。

留意点●裏突き。床と平行、伸ばしすぎない。

着眼点●西（体は北）

1: Pull down right foot toward east.
2: Shikodachi
3: Left-Chudan-Uratsuki (Gyakuken). Right hand to Kaisho, with fingers pointing upward, hold it in front of abdomen (Osaeuke).
4: West (body faces north)

Point: Uratsuki. Keep parallel with floor and do not push out too much.

挙動の分解7　Seipai Kumite in detail

㉕

16挙動

⑤⑨

足の動作●右足を軸に体を右へ回転（90°）させ、東向き。右足前三戦立ち。
立ち方●右三戦立ち。
手の動作●右中段掛け受け。左は開掌で甲を上に左脇に構える。

着眼点●東

⑥⓪

足の動作●体をひねり右足前、半後屈立ちとなる。
立ち方●半後屈立ち。
手の動作●右半打拳にて下段打ち。左開掌は握りながら左脇に構える。

着眼点●東（体は北）

⑥①

足の動作●⑥⓪のまま。
立ち方●半後屈立ち。
手の動作●右上段裏拳打ち。体、左拳はそのまま。

着眼点●東（体は北）

1:Pivoing on right foot, turn body 90 degree toward right, facing east.
2:Sanchindachi (right foot in front)
3:Right-Chudan-Kakeuke. Left hand to Kaisho, with back of hand facing upward, hold it under left armpit.
4:East

1:Twist body.
2:Half-Kokutsudachi (right foot in front)
3:Gedan-Uchi with right Half-Daken. Clenching left hand Kaisho, hold it under left armpit.
4:East (body faces north)

1:Same as in ⑥⓪.
2:Half-Kokutsudachi
3:Right-Jyodan-Uraken-Uchi. Body and left fist remain the same.
4:East (body faces north)

17挙動

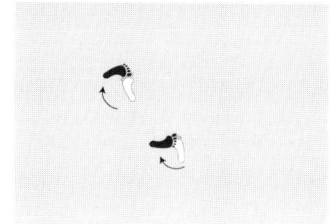

足の動作●体を東の方向に捻り、右足前三戦立ちにもどる。
立ち方●右三戦立ち。
手の動作●左中段横受け。右拳は右脇に構える。

着眼点●東

1: Twist body toward east, returning to Sanchindachi.
2: Sanchindachi (right foot in front)
3: Left-Chudan-Yokouke. Hold right fist under right armpit.
4: East

足の動作●左中段前蹴り。
立ち方●片足立ち。
手の動作●手の構えはそのまま。

着眼点●東

1: Left-Chudan-Maegeri
2: Stand on right foot.
3: Same as in ㊻.
4: East

18挙動

足の動作●左足を西の方向に引き、四股立ちとなる。
立ち方●四股立ち。
手の動作●右中段裏突き（逆拳）。左手は開掌、指先を上に水月の前に構える（押え受け）。

着眼点●東（体は北）

1: Pull down left foot toward west to stand Shikodachi.
2: Shikodachi
3: Right-Chudan-Uratsuki (Gyakuken). Left hand Kaisho, with fingers pointing upward, hold it in front of abdomen (Osaeuke).
4: East (body faces north)

セーパイ

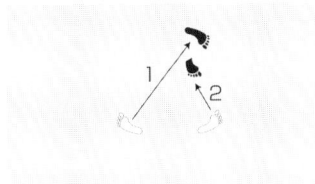

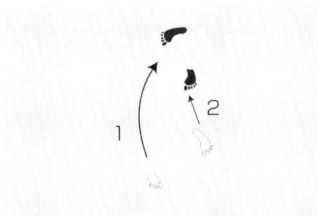

足の動作●左足を北方向に１歩進め、左足を軸に体を南方向に回転（180°）右足を寄せて右足前猫足立ちとなる。
立ち方●右猫足立ち。
手の動作●両手を開掌にして、掌を向かい合わせて水月の前に構える（右手上、左手下）、天地の構え。

留意点●両手は前に突き出さない

着眼点●南

1: Take left foot one step toward north. Pivoting on left foot, turn body 180 degree toward south. Pull right foot together.
2: Nekoashidachi to stand Nekoashidachi
3: Both hands Kaisho, facing palms each other, hold them in front of abdomen (right hand above, left hand below).
4: South

Point: Don't thrust out both hands.

足の動作●右足を北方向に１歩引くと同時に左足を寄せて右足前猫足立ちとなる。
立ち方●右猫足立ち。
手の動作●両掌は向かい合わせたまま握りながら、円を描くように顔面辺りより右拳下、左拳が上になるようにねじり引き落とす。

留意点●両手は前方に伸ばさない。

着眼点●南

1: While pulling back right foot one step toward north slide left foot together to stand Nekoashidachi (left foot in front).
2: Nekoashidachi
3: With palms facing each other, clench both fists and drawing a circle in front of face, twist while pushing downward so that right fist comes to the bottom and left fist on top.
4: South

Point: Don't stretch out both hands.

拳動の分解19　Seipai Kumite in detail

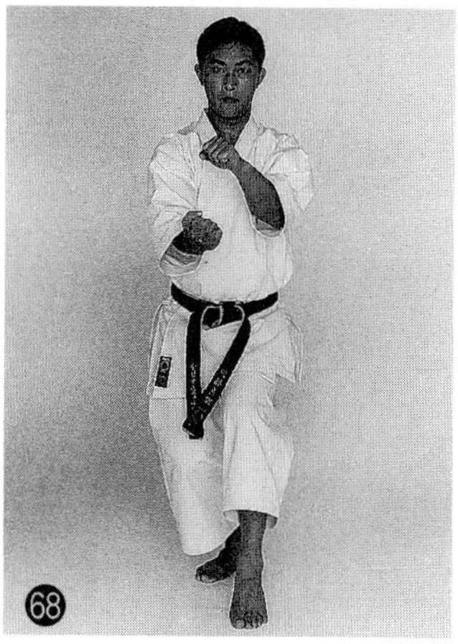
68

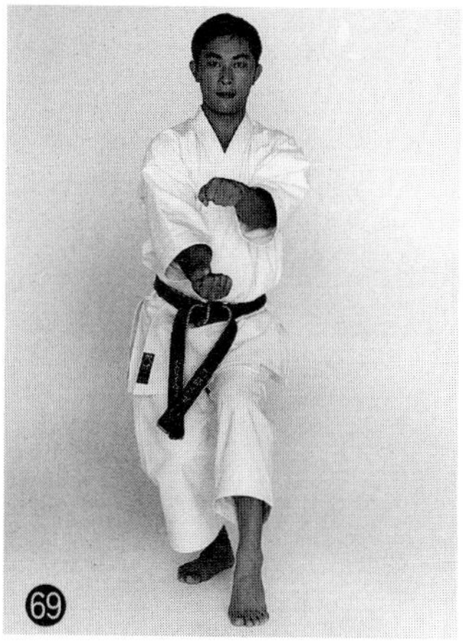
69

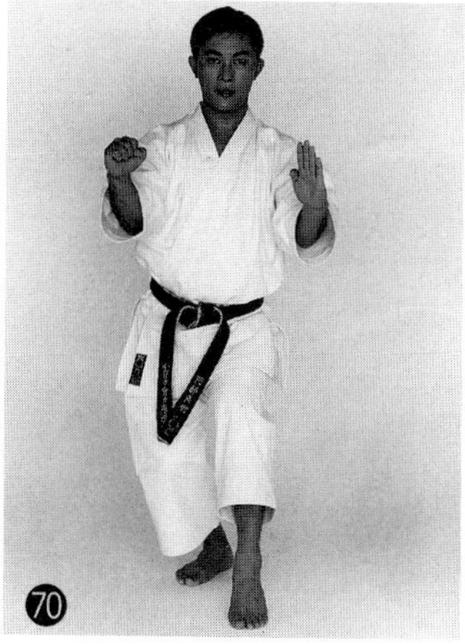
70

19挙動

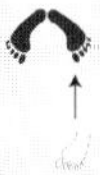

足の動作●⓺⓼のまま。
立ち方●左猫足立ち。
手の動作●右拳槌、左開掌にて下段回し打ちをする。

着眼点●南

足の動作●左足を右手に引きつけ、結び立ちとなる。
立ち方●結び立ち。
手の動作●右手は握り左手は開掌にして右拳を上、左掌を下に重ね、回すように金的の前に重ねて構える（左手前、右手後ろ）次いで右拳を開く。

着眼点●南

1: Same as in ⓺⓼.
2: Nekoashidachi (left foot in front)
3: With right hand Kentsui and left hand Kaisho, execute Gedan-Mawashiuchi.
4: South

1: Bringing back left foot to right foot, return to Musubidachi.
2: Musubidachi
3: While clenching right palm and left hand Kaisho with right fist top and left palm bottom facing each other, place in front of abdomen. Turning hands, invert so that left palm is now on top of right palm in front of Kinteki (groin).
4: South

挙動の分解19　Seipai Kumite in detail

20挙動　止め（直立）

⑭　⑮

足の動作●結び立ち。
立ち方●結び立ち。
手の動作●両手は開いて大腿部両側に付けて伸す。

着眼点●南

1:Musubidachi
2:Musubidachi
3:Open both hands and extend down the stretched arms.
4:South

サイファ篇

〔特徴〕

サイファは短かい形であるが立ち方の種類が多くまた剛柔流の特徴のある技が多く含まれている。各立ち方の正確さと移動のスムースさが求められ手技とのバランスが大切である。

Though being a short Kata, SAIFA contains various types of stances, as well as major techniques of the Goju-ryu style. Smoothness of movements, precise technique, as well as balance are emphasized.

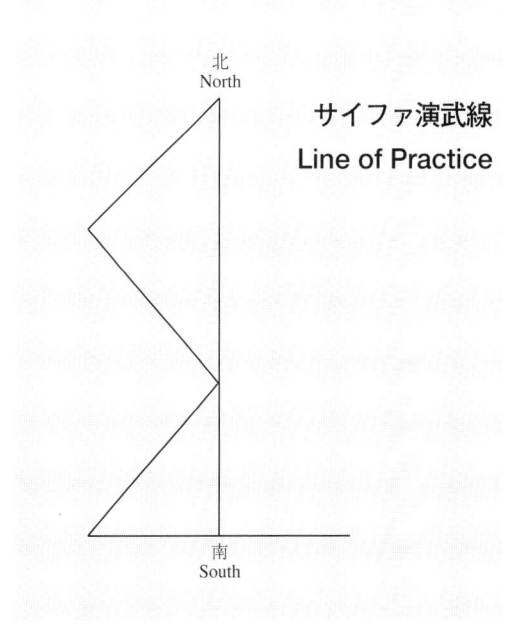

サイファ演武線
Line of Practice

SAIFA

直立　　　　　用意　　　　　1 挙動

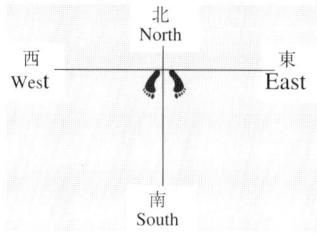

足の動作●結び立ち。
立ち方●結び立ち。
手の動作●両手は開いて大腿部両側に付けて伸す。

足の動作●結び立ち。
立ち方●結び立ち。
手の動作●両手を開き金的の前に構える（左手上、右手下）。

着眼点●南（正面やや高め）

足の動作●両爪先を軸に平行立ちとなる。
立ち方●平行立ち。
手の動作●両手を握りながら両体側へ手の甲を外側に構える（丹田を中心に全身に力を入れる）。

留意点●膝が伸び、棒立ちにならない様注意。

着眼点●南

Remarks
1:Feet
2:Stance
3:Hands
4:Point to see

1:Musubidachi
2:Musubidachi
3:Open both hands and extend down the stretched arms.

1:Musubidachi
2:Musubidachi
3:Open both hands, place them in front of Kinteki (groin), with left hand on top of right hand.
4:South (slightly upward)

1:Pivoting on the toes, move both heels outward until parallel.
2:Heikodachi
3:Clenching the fists, move them to the sides of the body, with back of the hand facing outwards.
4:South
Point:Pay attention that knees do not stand upright.

サイファ

【❺を東から見る】
❺ seen from east.

【❼を東から見る】
❼ seen from east.

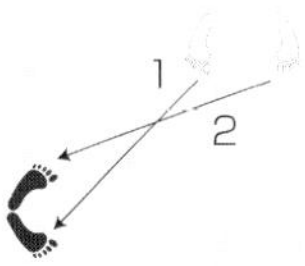

足の動作●右足を南西の方向に1歩進め、左足を引きつけ東向き、結び立ちとなる。
立ち方●結び立ち。
手の動作●右縦拳を右脇にあげ、左手は縦拳部を握る。
留意点●移動は摺り足で、腰が上下しないようにする。
着眼点●東

1: Take right foot one step toward southwest, then, pulling left foot together, face east to stand Musubidachi.
2: Musubidachi
3: Lift Right-Tateken up to right armpit, grasp Right-Tateken with Left hand.
4: East
Point: Move with a sliding step while avoiding up and down movements of the hips.

足の動作●❹のまま。
立ち方●結び立ち。
手の動作●❹が終わると同時に左手は右拳を握ったまま右拳を左乳下へ振りきるように移動させる。
留意点●左に寄せる時力強く素早くする。
着眼点●東

1: Same as in ❹.
2: Musubidachi
3: As soon as finishing ❹, while left hand clasping right fist, swing right fist with force toward lower left side of the breast.
4: East

Point: Move swiftly and forcefully when left hand draws lower left side of breast.

挙動の分解1　Saifa Kumite in detail

▶サイファ篇　33

2 挙動

⑨

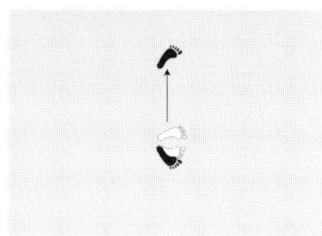

【⑨を東から見る】
⑨ seen from east.

⑩

⑪

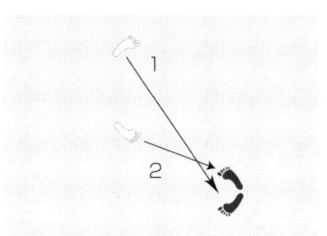

足の動作●左足を北の方向に引き、四股立ちとなる。
立ち方●四股立ち。
手の動作●右上段裏拳打ち。左手は顔面辺りより指先を上に水月の前に構える（押え受け）。

留意点●手首がしっかり返っているか注意（スナップ）。

着眼点●南（体は東）

1: Pull left foot back toward north to stand Shikodachi
2: Shikodachi
3: Right-Jyodan-Uraken-Uchi. With fingers pointing upward, move left hand from around the height of face to front of abdomen (Osaeuke).
4: South (body faces east)

Point: Be sure to snap the wrist.

足の動作●左足を南東の方向に1歩進め、右足を引きつけ、西向き結び立ちとなる。
立ち方●結び立ち。
手の動作●左縦拳を左脇にあげ、右手で縦拳部を握る。

着眼点●西

1: Take left foot one step toward southeast, then, pulling right foot together, face west to be Musubidachi.
2: Musubidachi
3: Lift left Tateken up to left armpit, grasp Left-Tateken with right hand.
4: West

挙動の分解1　Saifa Kumite in detail

④

サイファ

3 挙動

⑫ ⑬ ⑭ ⑮

【⑭を西から見る】
⑭ seen from west.

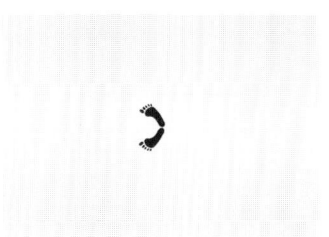

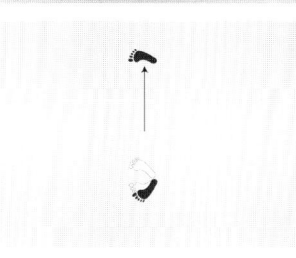

足の動作●⑫のまま。
立ち方●結び立ち。
手の動作●⑪が終わると同時に右手は左拳を握ったまま右乳下へ振りきるように移動させる。

着眼点●西

足の動作●右足を北の方向に引き、四股立ちとなる。
立ち方●四股立ち。
手の動作●左上段裏拳打ち。右手は顔面辺りより指先を上に水月の前に構える(押え受け)。

着眼点●南(体は西)

1:Same as in ⑫.
2:Musubidachi
3:As soon as finishing ⑪, swing left fist with force toward lower right side of breast, while still placing right hand grips left fist.
4:West

1:Pull back right foot toward north to be Shikodachi.
2:Shikodachi.
3:Left-Jyodan-Uraken-Uchi. With fingers pointing upward, move right hand from around the height of face to front of abdomen (Osaeuke).
4:South (body faces west)

4 挙動

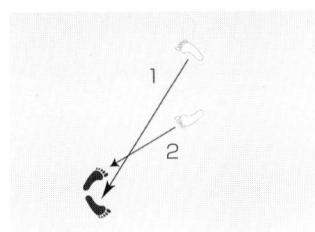

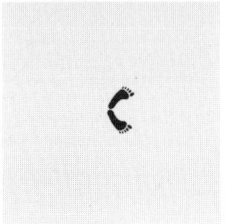

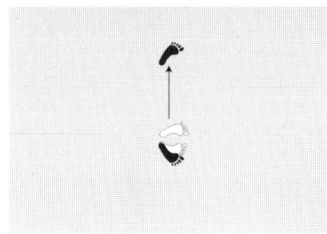

❶ ❷ ❸ ❹

❹に同じ。
Same as in ㉛.

❺に同じ。
Same as in ❺.

❼に同じ。
Same as in ❼.

❾に同じ。
Same as in ❾.

サイファ

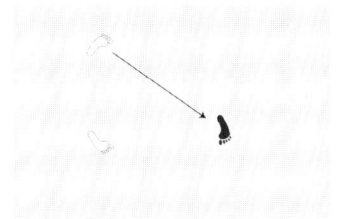

足の動作●左足を右足の東の方向へ１歩出し、右膝当て。
立ち方●左片足立ち。爪先を下げる。
手の動作●左中段すくい掛け受け（開掌）、右下段押え受け（開掌）。

留意点●両手でバランスをとる肘が外へ出ないようにしめる。肩に力が入らない様にする。

着眼点●西（体は西）

1: Step towards the east with left foot, execute Right-Hizaate.
2: Stand on left foot.
3: Left-Chudan-Sukui-Kakeuke with Kaisho. Right-Gedan-Osaeuke with Kaisho.
4: West (body faces south)

Point: Maintain hand position throughout the movement. and don't stiffen shoulders.

足の動作●右膝当て（⑳）より右中段前蹴り。
立ち方●左片足立ち。
手の動作●⑳のまま。

備考●蹴る瞬間南を向く。

着眼点●南

1: Right Hizaate (as in ⑳), then, Right-Chudan-Maegeri.
2: Standing on left foot.
3: Same as in ⑳.
4: South

Note: Face toward south at the moment of kick.

挙動の分解 5　Saifa Kumite in detail

▶サイファ篇　37

足の動作●右足を左足の西の方向へ1歩出し、左膝当て。
立ち方●右片足立ち。爪先を下げる。
手の動作●右中段すくい掛け受け（開掌）。左下段押え受け（開掌）。

着眼点●東（体は南）

足の動作●左膝当て（㉓）より左中段前蹴り。
立ち方●右片足蹴り。
手の動作●㉓のまま。
備考●蹴る瞬間南を向く

着眼点●南

足の動作●蹴った左足を北の方向に引き、右足前、前屈立ちとなる。
立ち方●右前屈立ち。
手の動作●開掌の両手は握りながら甲を上に両脇に引きつけ、肩よりやや高く、肩幅よりやや広く正拳、双手（両手）突き。

着眼点●南

1: Taking right foot one step toward west of left foot, execute Left-Hizaate.
2: Stand on right foot.
3: Right-Chudan-Sukui-Kakeuke with Kaisho. Left-Gedan-Osaeuke with Kaisho.
4: East (body faces south)

1: Left-Hizaate (as in ㉓), then, Left-Chudan-Maegeri.
2: Kick with right foot.
3: Same as in ㉓.
4: South

Note: Face toward south at the moment of kick.

1: After kicking, pull back left foot toward north.
2: Zenkutsudachi to stand Zenkutsudachi.
3: While clenching both hands, pull them under the armpits with the back of the hands facing upwards. Then execute Seiken-Morotetsuki with arms a little wider than shoulder width, and a little higher than shoulder height excute Morote-Tsuki with Seiken.
4: South

5 挙動

⑳ ㉘ ㉙ ㉚

【㉘から㉚を北から見る】
㉘㉚ seen from north.

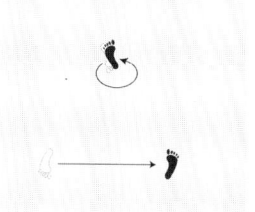

足の動作●㉕のまま。
立ち方●右前屈立ち。
手の動作●両拳は半円を描くように右拳は拳槌。左拳は開きながら体の中心部前、右膝上縦拳で２つ位の高さ辺を打つ。
留意点●左右の手は肘関節を支点に前腕部だけで円を描くように回す（両肘を軸に）。

着眼点●南

1: Same as in ㉕.
2: Zenkutsudachi (right foot in front)
3: Draw a semi-circle with both hands and execute Right-Kentsui striking the open left palm at a position in the front center of the body at a height of two Tateken higher than knee level.
4: South

Point: Both hands turn like drawing a circle fulcruming joint of elbow (making elbows axis)

足の動作●右足を東へ、左足の前を通り交差させると同時に体を左回転させて北の方向を向く。
立ち方●左前屈立ち。
手の動作●両手を開拳にして、胸の前で交叉させるように左振り受け（掛け受け）をしながら甲を上に両拳を両脇に引きつけ、肩よりやや高く、肩幅よりやや広く正拳両手突き。

着眼点●北

1: Step right foot toward east in front of left foot and, while crossing with left foot, turn body toward left, facing north.
2: Zenkutsudachi (left foot in front)
3: Both hands to Kaisho and, in a crossing movement in front of chest, execute Left-Furiuke (Kakeuke), at the same time, pull both fists under armpits with back of hands facing upward, executing Morotetsuki with Seiken.
4: North

挙動の分解6　*Saifa Kumite in detail*

⑥ ⑦

▶サイファ篇　39

6 挙動

足の動作●㉚のまま。
立ち方●左前屈立ち。
手の動作●両拳は半円を描くように左拳は拳槌、右拳は開きながら体の中心部、左膝上縦拳で2つ位の高さ辺を打つ。

着眼点●北

1: Same as in ㉚.
2: Zenkutsudachi (left foot in front)
3: Draw a semi-circle with both hands and end with Left-Kentsui striking the open right palm at a position in the front center of the body at a height two Tateken higher than knee level.
4: North

挙動の分解7　Saifa Kumite in detail

サイファ

7挙動

足の動作●右足は内側に足払い、体を東の方向に回転させる。
立ち方●平行立ち。
手の動作●右上段拳槌打ち。左拳は脇に構える。

留意点●着地と拳槌打ちが同時になるようにする。
「エイ」の気合を掛け、頭頂部を打つ。

着眼点●南（体は東）

1: Execute Ashibarai with right foot to the inside, and, using the momentum, rotate body toward east.
2: Heikoudachi
3: Right-Jyodan-Kentsuiuchi. Hold left fist under left armpit.
4: South (body faces east)

Point: Kentsuiuchi and the landing of the foot should be done simultaneously. Strike opponent's top of head, with Kiai crying out "Ei".

足の動作●❸のまま。
立ち方●平行立ち。
手の動作●右拳槌はその位置で手の甲を上にして開掌、その開掌を指先に力を入れながら甲が上のまま右脇に引く。左拳は中段裏突き。

留意点●体は東のまま腰を使い、裏突きをする。

着眼点●南

1: Same as in ❸.
2: Heikodachi
3: Positioning right hand unchanged, open Kentsui to Kaisho, with back of hand facing upward, then, gripping the tips of fingers, pull it under right armpit, with back of hand still facing upward. Execute Chudan-Uratsuki with left fist.
4: South

Point: Using the hips, execute Uratsuki, maintaining body position toward the east.

挙動の分解7　Saifa Kumite in detail

8 挙動

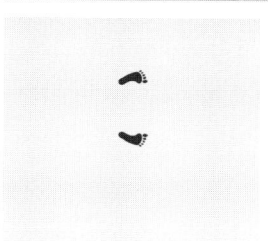

足の動作●左足は内側に足払い。
立ち方●平行立ち。
手の動作●左上段拳槌打ち。右拳は右脇に構える。

着眼点●北（体は東）

足の動作●⓵のまま。
立ち方●平行立ち。
手の動作●左拳槌はその位置で手の甲を上にして開掌、その開掌を指先に力を入れながら甲が上のまま左脇に引く。右拳は中段裏突き。

着眼点●北

1: Execute Ashibarai with left foot to the inside.
2: Heikodachi
3: Left-Jyodan-Kentsuiuchi. Hold right fist under right armpit.
4: North (body faces east)

1: Same as in ⓵.
2: Heikodachi.
3: Position of left hand unchanged, open Kentsui to Kaisho, with back of hand facing upward, then, gripping the tips of fingers, pull it under left armpit, with back of hand still facing upward. Execute Chudan Uratsuki with right fist.
4: North

サイファ

9 挙動

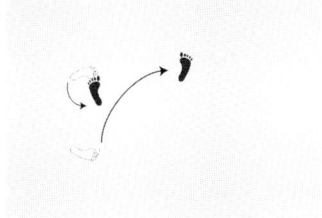

足の動作●右足を北の方向に進め、右足前三戦立ち。
立ち方●右三戦立ち。

着眼点●北

手の動作●左拳は甲を上にした構えより肩の高さへ正拳突き。右拳は右脇に構える。

1: Step right foot forward to north.
2: Sanchindachi (right foot in front)
3: Keeping back of hand facing upward, execute Chudan-Seikentsuki with left fist toward shoulder height level. Hold right fist under right armpit.
4: North

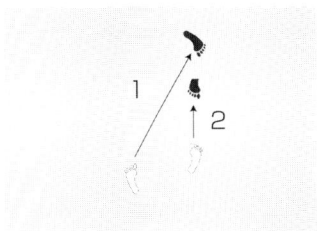

足の動作●左足を右足前(北)へ1歩踏み出し、体を右に半回転(180°)させて右足前猫足立ちとなる。
立ち方●右猫足立ち。
手の動作●左手は掌を上にして左脇に構える(開掌)。右手は開き、右裏手刀外回し打ち(背刀打ち)、左開掌の上に構える。

着眼点●南

1: Take left foot a step in front of right foot toward north, then, turn body 180 degree toward right.
2: Nekoashidachi (right foot in front)
3: Hold left hand Kaisho under left armpit, with palm facing upward. Open right hand and, executing side blow attack with Right-Urashuto (Haito-Uchi), hold it above Left-Kaisho.
4: South

挙動の分解10　Saifa Kumite in detail

サイファ篇　43

10挙動

足の動作●❺⓪のまま。
立ち方●右猫足立ち。
手の動作●左右回し受け。右手は上より円を描くように指先を下に向け右脇に構える。左手脇の位置で回し指先を上に向け左脇に構える。

着眼点●南

足の動作●❺⓪のまま。
立ち方●右猫足立ち。
手の動作●左手は肩の高さ、指先を上、掌底で大胸筋、右掌底で鼠蹊部を押す。

留意点●両掌とも、出来るだけ正面に向ける。

着眼点●南

1: Same as in ❺⓪.
2: Nekoashidachi (right foot in front)
3: Execute Mawashiuke with both hands, by drawing right hand as if making a circle in front of face and bring it under right armpit, with fingers pointing down ward. At the same time, point the fingers of the left hand upward by twisting the wrist clockwise with fingers pointing upward.
4: South

1: Same as in ❺⓪.
2: Nekoashidachi (right foot in front)
3: Left hand is at shoulder height, with fingers pointing upward, push opponent's chest muscle with Left-Shotei, while also pushing opponent's groin with Right-Shotei.
4: South
Point: Both palms face front as much as possible.

サイファ

11挙動　止め（直立）

足の動作●右足を左足に引きつける。
立ち方●結び立ち。
手の動作●両手は右掌を上、左掌を下に重ね、回すように金的の前に重ねて構える（左手前、右手後ろ）。

着眼点●南

足の動作●結び立ち。
立ち方●結び立ち。
手の動作●両手は開いて大腿部両側に付けて伸ばす。

着眼点●南

1: Pull right foot to left foot until heels come together.
2: Musubidachi
3: With the right hand on top, bring both hands together. Then turning both hands inward move them to the front of the groin with the left hand on top.
4: South

1: Musubidachi
2: Musubidachi
3: Open both hands and stretch both sides of thighs.
4: South

ジオン篇

〔特徴〕

おだやかな動きの中に激しい気魂のこもった形である。転進、転回、寄り足などを体得するのに適している形である。

練習に際しては特にむずかしい技はないが、平安、鉄騎の中にある種々の立ち方、技を正確に使って緩急のリズム、方向転換の際の手脚同時の基礎的動きが大切であり基本技を大変重んじた形である。

JION is KATA of calm movement combined with vibrant power. It is an ideal KATA for mastering techniques that require changing direction, rotating, Yoriashi (moving from the front foot), and so forth. In practice, there are no especially difficult techniques in this KATA. However, a lot of emphasis is placed on the accurate use of basic techniques including stances (also found in Heian and Tekki), techniques employing quick/slow rhythm, and techniques using simultaneous movement of hand and foot while changing direction.

※従来の外受けを内受けに、内受けを外受けに統一した。
※Traditional Sotouke is changed into Uchiuke and Uchiuke is changed into Sotouke respectively.

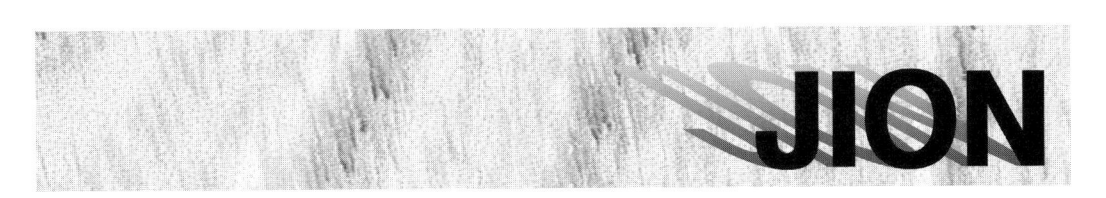

JION

直立　　　　　　　　用意　　　　　　　　1挙動

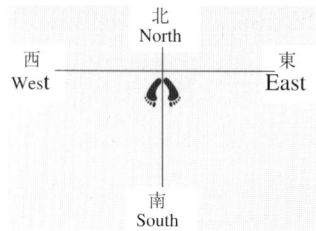

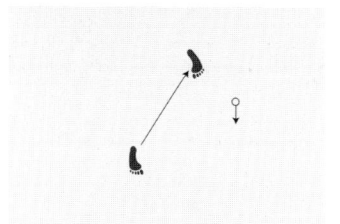

足の動作●結び立ち。
立ち方●結び立ち。
手の動作●両手は開いて大腿部両側に付けて伸ばす。

足の動作●結び立ちから閉足立ちとなる。
立ち方●閉足立ち。
手の動作●右拳を左拳で包み、下顎前に拳2つくらい離して構える。両肘の間隔は肩幅程度。

足の動作●左足を北に引く。
立ち方●右前屈立ち。
手の動作●両拳を胸前で交差させて右中段外受け。同時に左下段受けを行う。

留意点●挙動1—12前屈立ちに注意する。後足の張りが悪く、足刀部が床面に密着しないことのないように。挙動2—3中段搔分けより前蹴りの時の拳の位置は、そのまま。

着眼点●南　　　　　　　　　　　　着眼点●南

Remarks
1:Feet
2:Stance
3:Hands
4:Point to see

1:Musubidachi
2:Musubidachi
3:Open both hands and stretch down both sides of thighs.

1:Move from Musubidachi to Heisokudachi
2:Heisokudachi
3:Wrapping right fist with left palm, hold hands in front of lower part of jaw about two fists distance away. Space between both elbows is about shoulder width.
4:South

1:Pull back left foot toward north.
2:Right-Zenkutsudachi
3:After crossing both fists in front of the the chest, execute Right-Chudan-Sotouke. At the same time, execute Left-Gedanuke.
4:South

Musubidachi must be formed before Yo-i position.
Point: Motion 1-12 In Zenkutudachi position, edge of back foot must stick to the floor.
Point: Motion 2-3 Fist position same at Maegeri as after Chudan-Kakiwake.

ジ オ ン

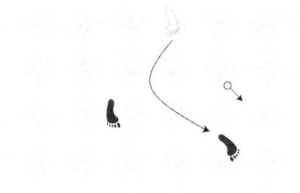

2 挙動　　3 挙動

備考●前屈立ち。前足の指先の方向と後足の方向は同じ方向。両足が床面に密着すること（特に後足の足刀部）。

足の動作●左足を1歩南東にすり出す。
立ち方●左前屈立ち。
手の動作●両拳を胸前で交差して（右手・手前）ゆっくりしぼりながら両拳中段掻分け受け。（甲斜め上）。

着眼点●南東

足の動作●南東に右中段前蹴り。
立ち方●左脚立ち。
手の動作●❺のまま。

備考●挙動3―4は連続して行う。

着眼点●南東

Note: Zenkutsudachi. Both toes of front and back foot point in same direction. Both feet must stick to floor (Especially the edge of the back foot).

1: Slide left foot one step out toward southeast.
2: Left-Zenkutsudachi
3: After crossing both fists (right hand inside) slowly, spread and hold them at Chudan-Kakiwakeuke, with back of hands facing diagonally upward.
4: Southeast

1: Right-Chudan-Maegeri to southeast.
2: Stand on left foot.
3: Same as in ❺.
4: Southeast

Note: Motion 3-4 must be done continuously.

▶ジオン篇　49

4 挙動

足の動作●右足を南東におろす。
立ち方●右前屈立ち。
手の動作●右中段順突き。左拳は左腰に引く。

着眼点●南東

1: Put down right foot toward southeast.
2: Right-Zenkutsudachi
3: Right-Chudan-Juntsuki. Pull back left fist to the left hip.
4: Southeast

5 挙動

足の動作●❼のまま。
立ち方●❼のまま。
手の動作●左中段逆突き。右拳は右腰に引く。

着眼点●南東

1: Same as in ❼.
2: Right-Zenkutsudachi
3: Left-Chudan-Gyakutsuki. Pull back right fist to the right hip.
4: Southeast

6 挙動

足の動作●❼のまま。
立ち方●❼のまま。
手の動作●連続して右中段順突き。左拳は左腰に引く。

備考●5—6挙動は連続して行う。

着眼点●南東

1: Same as in ❼.
2: Right-Zenkutsudachi
3: Execute Right-Chudan-Juntsuki continuously. Pull back left fist to left hip.
4: Southeast

Note: Motion 5-6 must be done continuously.

ジオン

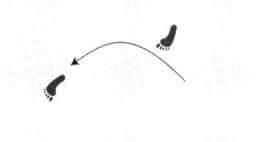

7 挙動　　　8 挙動

足の動作●右足を南西にすり出す。
立ち方●右前屈立ち。
手の動作●両拳を胸前で交差して（右手、手前）ゆっくりしぼりながら両拳中段搔分け受け（甲斜め上）。

着眼点●南西

足の動作●南西に左中段前蹴り。
立ち方●右脚立ち。
手の動作●⓫のまま。

備考●8―9挙動は連続して行う。

着眼点●南西

1:Slide right foot out toward southwest.
2:Right-Zenkutsudachi
3:After crossing both fists(right hand inside) in front of the chest,execute Chudan-Kakiwakeuke while twisting both fists slowly (back of fists facing diagonally upwards),
4:Southwest

1:Left-Chudan-Maegeri toward southwest.
2:Stand on the right foot.
3:Same as in ⓫.
4:Southwest

Note: Motion 8-9 must be done continuously.

▶ジオン篇　51

9挙動　　　　　　　10挙動　　　　　　　11挙動

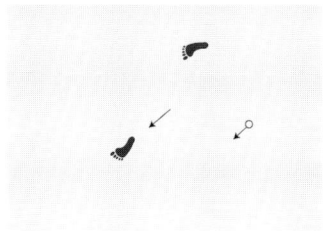

足の動作●左足を南西におろす。
立ち方●左前屈立ち。
手の動作●左中段順突き。右拳は右腰に引く。

着眼点●南西

足の動作●⑬のまま。
立ち方●⑬のまま。
手の動作●右中段逆突き。左拳は左腰に引く。

着眼点●南西

足の動作●⑬のまま。
立ち方●⑬のまま。
手の動作●連続して左中段順突き。右拳は右腰に引く。

備考●10―11挙動は連続して行う。

着眼点●南西

1: Put down left foot toward southwest.
2: Left-Zenkutsudachi
3: Left-Chudan-Juntsuki. Pull back right fist to the right hip.
4: Southwest

1: Same as in ⑬.
2: Left-Zenkutsudachi
3: Right-Chudan-Gyakutsuki. Pull back left fist to the left hip.
4: Southwest

1: Same as in ⑬.
2: Left-Zenkutsudachi
3: Execute Left-Chudan-Juntsuki continuously. Pull back right fist to the right hip.
4: Southwest

Note: Motion 10-11 must be done continuously.

12挙動　　　13挙動　　ジオン

⑯　⑰　⑱

足の動作●左足を南に移動させる（⑯途中の姿勢止まらない）。
立ち方●左前屈立ち。（半身）
手の動作●左足を正面又は南に移しながら右手をいったん額前に上げ、左拳は左腰から左前屈立と同時に左上段揚受け。右拳は右腰に引く。

着眼点●南

足の動作●⑰のまま。
立ち方●⑰のまま。
手の動作●右中段逆突き。左拳は左腰に引く。

留意点●上段揚受けの時半身の姿勢をとる。腰の回転を充分に12―13挙動は連続して行なう。

着眼点●南

1:Move left foot foward south. (⑯ Shows form during the move. Do not stop at this point.)
2:Left-Zenkutsudachi (Hips in Hanmi position)
3:While moving left foot right hand lifts up in front of forehead, then, left fist lifts up from the left hip and Jyodan-Ageuke is executed at the same time as Left-Zenkutsudachi.Pull back right fist to the right hip.
4:South

1:Same as in ⑰.
2:Left-Zenkutsudachi
3:Right-Chudan-Gyakutsuki. Pull back left fist to the left hip.
4:South

Point:At Jyodan-Ageuke, body angle is about 45 degree.Motion 12-13 must be done continuously.

▶ジオン篇　53

14挙動　　15挙動

⑲ 　⑳　㉑

足の動作●右足を南に進める。
立ち方●右前屈立ち。（半身）
手の動作●右足を進めながら左手をいったん額前に上げ、右拳は右腰から右前屈立ちと同時に、右上段揚受け。左拳は左腰に引く。
備考●挙動14―15は連続して行う。
（⑲は途中止まらない）

着眼点●南

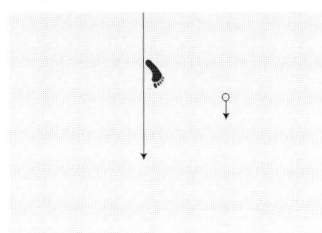

足の動作●⑳のまま。
立ち方●⑳のまま。
手の動作●左中段逆突き。右拳は右腰に引く。

着眼点●南

1:Step right foot toward south.
2:Right-Zenkutsudachi (Hips in Hanmi position)
3:While stepping with right foot, lift up left hand in front of the forehead, then, lift up right fist from the right hip and execute Right-Jyodan-Ageuke at the same time as Right-Zenkutsudachi. Pull back left fist to the left hip.
4:South
Note:Motion 14-15 must be done continuously. (⑲ Shows form during the move. Do not stop at this point.)

1:Same as in ⑳.
2:Right-Zenkutsudachi
3:Left-Chudan-Gyakutsuki. Pull back right fist to right hip.
4:South

ジオン

16挙動　　17挙動

㉒　㉓　㉔

足の動作●左足を南に進める。
立ち方●左前屈立ち。（半身）
手の動作●左足を進めながら右手をいったん額前に上げ、左拳は左腰から、左前屈立ちと同時に左上段揚受け。右拳は右腰に引く。
（㉒は途中止まらない）

着眼点●南

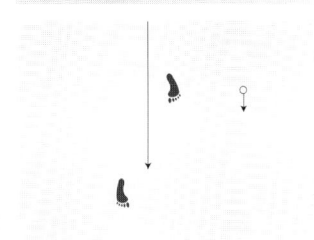

足の動作●右足を南に進める。
立ち方●右前屈立ち。
手の動作●右中段順突き。左拳は左腰に引く。

留意点●気合

着眼点●南

1: Step left foot toward south.
2: Left-Zenkutsudachi (Hips in Hanmi position)
3: While stepping out with left foot, lift up the right hand in front of the forehead, then, lift up left fist from the left hip and execute Jyodan - Ageuke at the same time as Left-Zenkutsudachi. Pull back right fist to the right hip. (㉒ Shows form during the move. Do not stop at this point.)
4: South

1: Step right foot toward south.
2: Right-Zenkutsudachi
3: Right-Chudan-Juntsuki. Pull back left fist to the left hip.
4: South

Point: Kiai.

18挙動

㉕
【㉖を北から見る】
㉖seen from north.

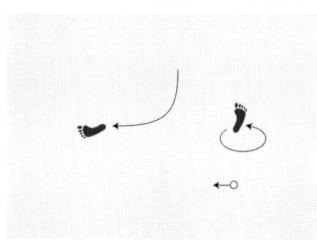

足の動作●右脚を軸に体を左に回転させ左足を西に移す。
立ち方●右後屈立ち。
手の動作●両腕をいったん胸前で交差し互いに引張り合うようにして、右拳右側面上段受け、左拳左側面下段受け。

留意点●後屈立ちで重心が前足にかかり過ぎない。重心の割合は後足7、前足3、のバランス。

着眼点●西

1: Pivoting right foot turn the body to left and bring left foot to west.
2: Right-Kokutsudachi
3: After crossing both fists in front of chest Sokumen-Jyodan-Uke with right fist and Left-Sokumen-Gedan-Uke with the left fist.
4: West

Point: At Kokutsudachi, don't put too much weight on the front foot. The balance of gravity should be 70% on the back foot and 30% on the front foot.

19挙動

㉗
【㉗を北から見る】
㉗seen from north.

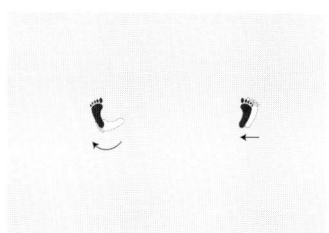

足の動作●左足を西に進め、右足を引きつける（寄り足）。
立ち方●騎馬立ち。
手の動作●右鉤突き。左拳は左腰に引く。

備考●右拳腰より。

着眼点●西

1: Step left foot toward west and drag the right foot (Yoriashi).
2: Kibadachi
3: Right-Kagitsuki. Pull back the left fist to the left hip.
4: West

Note: Right fist comes out from waist position

ジオン

20挙動

㉙ ㉚ ㉛ ㉜

【㉙を北から見る】
㉙seen from north.
備考●開掌の使い方もある

Note: Kaisho (open hand) can also be used.

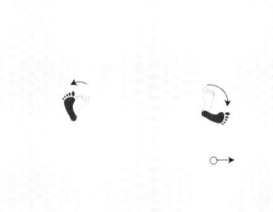

【㉛を北から見る】
㉛seen from north.

足の動作●東に向く。
立ち方●左後屈立ち。
手の動作●両拳をいったん胸前で交叉し互いに引張り合うようにして、左拳左側面上段受け。右拳右側面下段受け。㉕と反対姿勢。
（㉙は途中姿勢止まらない）
留意点●騎馬立ちから後屈立ちへ、後屈立ちから騎馬立ちへの変化があるが重心の移動が重要。

着眼点●東

1: Face east.
2: Left-Kokutsudachi
3: After crossing both fists in front of the chest Left-Sokumen-Jyodan-Uke with left fist and Right-Sokumen-Gedan-Uke with right fist. Opposite posture of ㉕. (㉙ Shows form during the move. Do not stop at this point.)
4: East
Point: In changing from Kibadachi to Kokutsudachi and Kokutsudachi to Kibadachi, movement of the centre of gravity is most important.

▶ジオン篇 57

21挙動

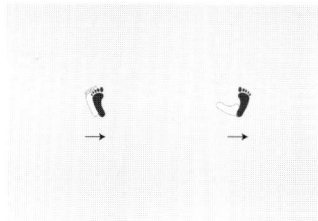

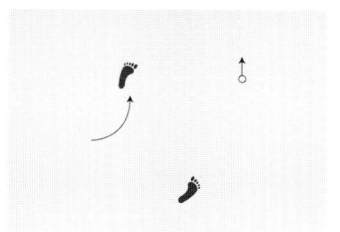

㉝

足の動作●右足を東に進め、左足を引きつける（寄り足）。
立ち方●騎馬立ち。
手の動作●左鉤突き。右拳は右腰に引く。

備考●左拳腰より。

着眼点●東

1:Step right foot toward east and drag the left foot (Yoriashi).
2:Kibadachi
3:Left-Kagitsuki. Pull back right fist to the right hip.
4:East

Note: Left fist comes out from the waist position.

22挙動

㉞ ㉟

足の動作●左足を北に進める。（㉞は途中の姿勢止まらない）
立ち方●左前屈立ち。（半身）
手の動作●左下段払い。右拳は右腰に引く。

着眼点●北

1:Step left foot torward north.
  (㉞ Shows form during the move. Do not stop at this point.)
2:Left-Zenkutsudachi (Hips in Hanmi position)
3:Left-Gedanbarai. Pull back right fist to the right hip.
4:North

23挙動

ジオン
24挙動

㊱

【㊱を西から見る】
㊱seen from west.

㊲

㊳

足の動作●右足を北に1歩進める。
立ち方●騎馬立ち。
手の動作●右側面右掌底中段横受け。左拳は左腰に引く。

着眼点●北

1:Take right foot one step toward north.
2:Kibadachi
3:Right-Side-Sokumen Right-Shotei and Chudan-Yokouke. Pull back left fist to the left hip.
4:North

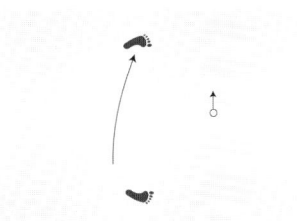

足の動作●左足を北に1歩進める。
立ち方●騎馬立ち。
手の動作●左側面左掌底、中段横受け。右拳は右腰に引く。

着眼点●北

1:Take left foot one step toward north.
2:Kibadachi
3:Left-side-Left-Shotei.Chudan-Yokouke.Pull back right fist to the right hip.
4:North

挙動の分解23　Jion Kumite in detail

中段順突きを（肘）右側面右掌底中段横受け。

①

Block Chudan-Jyuntsuki(elbow) with Right-side-Sokumen Right-Shotei Chudanyokouke.

▶ジオン篇　59

25挙動　　　　　　　　　　26挙動

備考●開掌の使い方もある

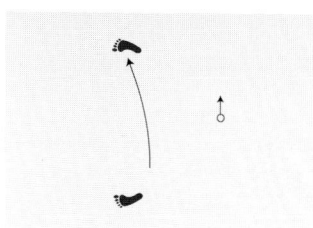

Note: Kaisho (open hand) can also be used.

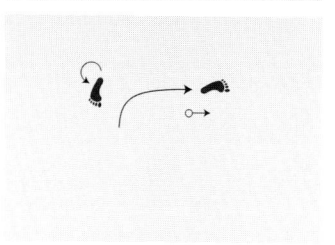

足の動作●右足を北に1歩進める。
立ち方●騎馬立ち。
手の動作●右側面右掌底、中段横受け。左拳は左腰に引く。

着眼点●北

足の動作●右脚を軸に体を左に回転させ左足を東に移す。
立ち方●右後屈立ち。
手の動作●両腕をいったん胸前で交差し互いに引張り合うようにして、右拳右側面上段受け、左拳左側面下段受け。㉕と同じ。
(㊵は途中姿勢止まらない)

着眼点●東

1: Move right foot one step toward north.
2: Kibadachi
3: Right-Side Right-Shotei. Chudan-Yokouke. Pull back left fist to the left hip.
4: North

1: Pivoting on right foot turn the body to the left and bring left foot toward east.
2: Right-Kokutsudachi
3: After crossing both fists in front of the chest while squeezing both arms, execute Sokumen-Jyodan-Uke with right fist and Left-Sokumen-Gedan-Uke with left fist(Same as in ㉕) (㊵ Shows form during the move. Do not stop at this point.)
4: East

27挙動

㊷ ㊸ ㊹

備考●開掌の使い方もある

Note: Kaisho (open hand) can also be used.

足の動作●左足に右足を引きつける。
立ち方●閉足立ち。
手の動作●左拳左側面上段諸手受け、右拳は左肘内側に添える（甲下向）。左肘は左肩の高さ。
（㊷㊹は途中の姿勢止まらない）

着眼点●東

1: Pull right foot to left foot.
2: Heisokudachi
3: Left-Sokumen-Jyodan-Moroteuke with left fist (back of hand facing downward) and place right fist inside of the left elbow. Left elbow is at height of the left shoulder.
(㊷ ㊹ Shows form before and after the move. Do not stop at these points.)
4: East

▶ジオン篇 61

28挙動　29挙動

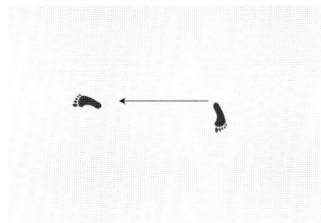

足の動作●右足を西に進める。
立ち方●左後屈立ち。
手の動作●両腕をいったん胸前で交差し、互いに引張り合うようにして、左拳左側面上段受け。右拳右側面下段受け。㉛と同じ。
（㊻は途中の姿勢止まらない）

着眼点●西

1:Step right foot toward west.
2:Left-Kokutsudachi
3:After crossing both fists in front of the chest, execute Left-Sokumen-Jyodan-Uke with left fist and Right-Sokumen-Gedan-Uke with right fist. Same as in ㉛.
（㊻ Shows form during the move. Do not stop at this point.)
4:West

足の動作●右足に左足を引きつける。
立ち方●閉足立ち。
手の動作●右拳右側面上段諸手受け。左拳は右肘内側に添える。（甲下向き。右肘は右肩の高さ）

着眼点●西

1:Pull left foot to the right foot.
2:Heisokudachi
3:Right-Sokumen-Jyodan-Moroteuke with right fist and place left fist (Right elbow is at height of the right shoulder) inside of the right elbow.
4:West

挙動の分解28　Jion Kumite in detail

左下段蹴りを右下段受けで内側から受ける。左側面上段受け。

Kumite for 28
Block opponent's Left-Gedangeri with Right-Gedan-Uke from inside. Left-side-Jyodan-Uke.

30挙動

㊽ ㊾ ㊿

足の動作●㊼のまま。
立ち方●㊼のまま。
手の動作●両拳両側に搔分け、おろしながら構える。
(㊽㊿は途中の姿勢止まらない)

着眼点●南

1: Same as in ㊼.
2: Heisokudachi
3: Spread both fists down to the both sides of the body and hold them there.
   (㊾ ㊿ Shows form before and after the move. Do not stop at these points.)
4: South

ジオン篇 63

31挙動　　32挙動

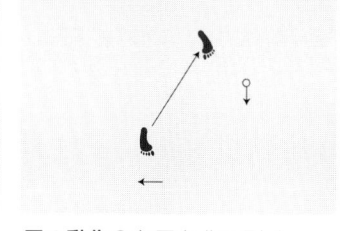

⑤51　⑤52　⑤53

足の動作●右足を南に大きく踏み込み、左足を引きつける。
立ち方●右足前交差立ち。
手の動作●両拳で下段交差受け。(右手上)。
留意点●交差立ちは、右足に左足を充分に引きつける。

着眼点●南

1: Take right foot a long step toward south, then, pull left foot together.
2: Right foot front Kosadachi
3: Gedan-Kosauke with both fists (right fist on top).
4: South
Point: At Kosadachi, pull right foot to the left foot closely.

足の動作●左足を北に引く。
立ち方●右前屈立ち。
手の動作●両拳を両側の下段へ掻分ける。

着眼点●南

1: Pull back left foot toward north.
2: Right-Zenkutsudachi
3: Spread fists down to the both sides of the body.
4: South

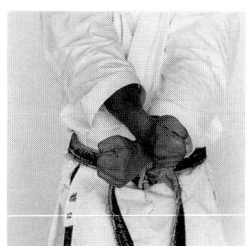

Note: position of hands.

64

33挙動

(54)

足の動作●左足を南に進める。
立ち方●左前屈立ち。
手の動作●両拳を胸前で交差（右手、手前）しながら両拳中段掻分け受け（両甲前向き）。
（(53)は途中の姿勢止まらない）
着眼点●南

1:Step left foot toward south.
2:Left-Zenkutsudachi
3:Crossing both fists in front of chest execute Chudan-Kakiwakeuke with both fists (back of both hands face front).
((53) Shows form during the move. Do not stop at this point.)
4:South

34挙動

(55)

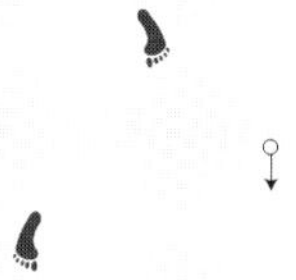

足の動作●右足を南に進める。
立ち方●右前屈立。
手の動作●両拳で上段交差受け（右手外）。

着眼点●南

1:Step right foot toward to south.
2:Right-Zenkutsudachi
3:Jyodan-Kosauke with both fists (right fist outside)
4:South

35挙動

(56)

(57)

【(56)を西から見る】
(56)seen from west.

足の動作●(55)のまま。
立ち方●(55)のまま。
手の動作●右上段裏拳打ち。左拳はそのまま。

留意点●写真(56)―(60)連続技なので敏速に続ける。

着眼点●南

1:Same as in (55).
2:Right-Zenkutsudachi
3:Execute Right-Jyodan-Uraken-Uchi Left fist stays where it is.
4:South

Point:Photo (56)-(60) are continuous techniques and must be done swiftly.

挙動の分解34、35 Jion Kumite in detail

右上段突きを右前屈立ちで上段交差受け。

③

Kumite for 34
Block opponent's Right-Jyodan tsuki with Jyodan-Kosauke in Right-Zenkutsu stance.

上段交差受けをし、ただちに右裏拳上段打ち。

④

Kumite for 35
Jyodan-Kosauke. Right-Uraken-Jyodan-Uchi immediately after Kosauke.

36挙動

⑤⑧

【⑤⑧を西から見る】
⑤⑧seen from west.

⑤⑨

足の動作●⑤⑤のまま。
立ち方●⑤⑤のまま。
手の動作●左拳中段突受け、右背腕上段流し受け。

着眼点●南

1: Same as in ⑤⑤.
2: Right-Zenkutsudachi
3: Execute Left-Fist-Chudan-Uke with Right Haiwan-Jyodan-Nagashiuke.
4: South

37挙動

⑥⓪

【⑥⓪を西から見る】
⑥⓪seen from west.

⑥①

足の動作●⑤⑤のまま。
立ち方●⑤⑤のまま。
手の動作●右上段裏拳打ち。同時に左腕は水月の前に添える。

着眼点●南

1: Same as in ⑤⑤.
2: Right-Zenkutsudachi
3: While executing Right-Jyodan-Uraken-Uchi, hold left arm in front of abdomen.
4: South

挙動の分解36、37　Jion Kumite in detail

⑤
すかさず左上段突きをするのを、右背腕上段流受け。

Kumiute for 36
When opponent attacks with Left-Jyodantsuki, immediately block with right Haiwan-Jyodan-Nagashiuke.

⑥
ただちに右裏拳打ちをする。同時に左腕は左手甲を右肘に接し、水月前に添える。

Kumite for 37
Counter immediately with Right-Jyodan-Uraken-Uchi, while placing left arm in front of abdomen. Back of left hand touches right elbow.

38挙動　39挙動

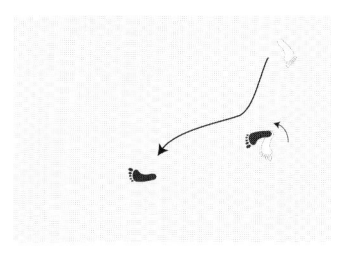

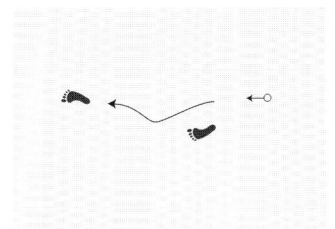

足の動作●右脚軸に体を左に回転させて左足を西に移動させる。
立ち方●左前屈立ち。（半身）
手の動作●左中段外受け。右拳は右腰に引く。
(㉖は途中の姿勢止まらない)

着眼点●西

足の動作●右足を西に1歩進める。
立ち方●右前屈立ち。
手の動作●右中段順突き。左拳は左腰に引く。

着眼点●西

1: Pivoting on the right foot turn the body to the left and bring left foot toward west.
2: Left-Zenkutsudachi (Hips in Hanmi position)
3: Left-Chudan-Sotouke. Pull back right fist to the right hip.
(㉖ Shows form during the move. Do not stop at this point.)
4: West

1: Take right foot one step toward west.
2: Right-Zenkutsudachi
3: Right-Chudan-Juntsuki. Pull back left fist to the left hip.
4: West

40挙動

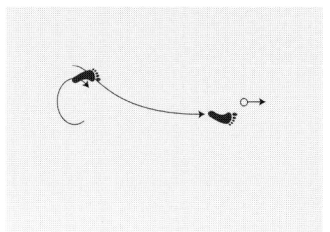

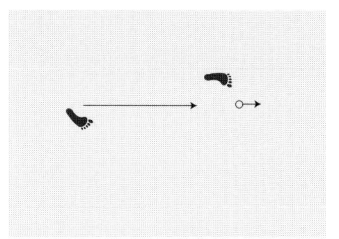

足の動作●体を右に回転させ右足を東に進める。
立ち方●右前屈立ち。(半身)
手の動作●右中段外受け。左拳は左腰に引く。
(⑥は途中の姿勢止まらない)

着眼点●東

1:Turn the body to the right and step right foot foward to east.
2:Right-Zenkutsudachi (Hips in Hanmi position)
3:Right-Chudan-Sotouke.
(⑥ Shows form during the move. Do not stop at this point.)
4:East

41挙動

足の動作●左足を東に1歩進める。
立ち方●左前屈立ち。
手の動作●左中段順突き。右拳は右腰に引く。

着眼点●東

1:Take left foot one step toward east.
2:Left-Zenkutsudachi
3:Left-Chudan-Juntsuki. Pull back right fist to the right hip.
4:East

42挙動

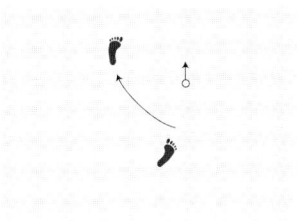

❻❽ ❻❾ ❼⓿

【❻❾を西から見る】
❻❾seen from west.

足の動作●左足を北へ移す。
立ち方●左前屈立ち。（半身）
手の動作●左下段払い。右拳は右腰に引く。

着眼点●北

1: Bring left foot toward north.
2: Left-Zenkutsudachi (Hips in Hanmi position)
3: Left-Gedanbarai. Right fist pulls back to the right hip.
4: North

▶ジオン篇 69

43挙動

⑦¹ ⑦² ⑦³

【⑦¹を西から見る】
⑦¹ seen from west.

足の動作●右膝を高くあげて北へ踏み込む。
立ち方●騎馬立ち。
手の動作●右拳は頭上高くふりあげ、右足を強く踏み込むと同時に、右拳右側面中段打落し。
(⑥⁹は途中の姿勢止まらない)
着眼点●北

1: Lift right knee up high, then, step in toward north.
2: Kibadachi
3: Lift right fist over head, then stamp right foot in strongly while executing right side Chudan-Uchiotoshi with the right fist.
   (⑥⁹ Shows form during the move. Do not stop at this point.)
4: North

挙動の分解43　Jion Kumite in detail

⑦
相手の中段順突きを右中段打落しで叩き落とす。

⑧
Kumite for ⑦²
Hit down opponent's Right-Chudantsuki with Right-Chudan-Uchiotoshi.

44挙動

45挙動

ジオン

足の動作●左膝を高くあげて北へ踏み込む。
立ち方●騎馬立ち。
手の動作●左拳は頭上高くふりあげ、左足を強く踏み込むと同時に左拳左側面中段打落し。⓫と反対姿勢。右拳は右腰に引く。
(⓭は途中の姿勢止まらない)

着眼点●北

足の動作●右膝を高くあげて北へ踏み込む。
立ち方●騎馬立ち。
手の動作●右拳は頭上高くふりあげ、右足を強く踏み込むと同時に右拳右側面中段打落し。⓫と同じ。左拳は左腰に引く。
(⓯は途中の姿勢止まらない)

着眼点●北

1: Lift left knee up high, then, step in toward north.
2: Kibadachi
3: Lift right fist over head, then stamp left foot in strongly while executing Left-side-Chudan-Uchiotoshi with left fist. (Opposite posture of ⓫.) Right fist pulls back to the right hip.
(⓭ Shows form during the move. Do not stop at this point.)
4: North

1: Lift right knee up to chest height, then, step in toward north.
2: kibadachi
3: Lift right fist over head, then stamp right foot in strongly while executing right side Chudan-Uchiotoshi with right fist. Same as in ⓫. Left fist pulls back to the left hip.
(⓯ Shows form during the move. Do not step at this point.)
4: North

▶ジオン篇 71

46挙動

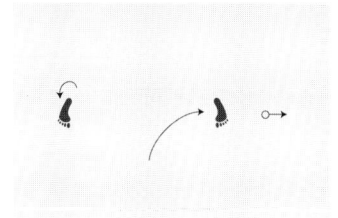

足の動作●右脚軸に体を左に回転させ左足を引きつけながら東へ移動させる（寄り足ぎみ）。

立ち方●騎馬立ち。

手の動作●体を回転させながら右掌は左肩前（東方からの中段突き）、左拳（甲上向き）は右脇。両腕を交差し、互いに引きしぼる。右拳右乳前（甲上向き）左拳左側面中段突き（甲上向き）。
（⑦は途中の姿勢止まらない）

着眼点●東

1. Pivoting right foot turn the body to the left, then, slide left foot to east (drag). (Similar to Yoriashi)
2. Kibadachi
3. While turning body, the right palm comes in front of the shoulder (Chudantsuki from east), pull back left fist (back of hand faces upward) to the right side of the body. Cross both arms and squeeze them inside. Right fist comes in front of the right breast (back of hand faces upward) and execute Left-side-Sokumen-Chudantsuki with left fist.
(⑦ Shows form during the move. Do not stop at this point.)
4. East

挙動の分解46　Jion Kumite in detail

相手の右中段順突きを右掌でつかみ、引き寄せながら、左拳左側面中段突き。

While taking hold of opponent's Right-Jyodan-Juntsuki and drawing with right palm, execute Left-Sokumen-Chudantsuki with left fist.

ジオン

47挙動 / 止め / 直立

⑧⓪ ⑧① ⑧②

北 North
西 West ── 東 East
南 South

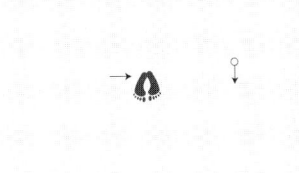

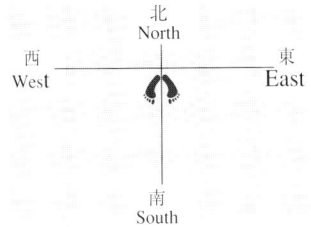

足の動作●右足を西に移し、左足を引きつける（寄り足）。
立ち方●騎馬立ち。
手の動作●顔を西（左）にむけると同時に左掌は右肩前（西方からの中段突き）右拳（甲上向き）は左脇。両腕を交差し、互いに引きしぼる。左拳は左乳前（甲上向き）、右拳は右側面中段突き（甲上向き）。

留意点●騎馬立ちで寄り足の時左足が流れないように。

留意点●気合
着眼点●西

1: Move right foot toward west, and, pull left foot drag (Yoriashi).
2: Kibadachi
3: While facing west (left), left palm comes in front of the shoulder, pull back right fist (back of hand faces upward) to the side body. Cross both arms and squeeze them inside. Right fist comes in front of the left breast (back of hand faces upward) and right side Chudantsuki (back of hand faces upward) with right fist.
4: East

Point: While standing Kibadachi position and in Yoriashi movement, left foot must not drift.

Point: kiai

足の動作●右足を左足に引きつける。
立ち方●閉足立ち。
手の動作●右拳を左拳で包み下顎前に構え、用意の姿勢にもどる。

備考●止めの時、残心に心がける。

着眼点●南

1: Pull right foot to the left foot.
2: Heisokudachi
3: Wrapping right fist with left palm, hold them in front of lower part of jaw, then return to Yo-i posture.
4: South

Note: At the position of Yame, a state of alertness is important.

足の動作●結び立ち。
立ち方●結び立ち。
手の動作●両手は開いて大腿部両側に付けて伸ばす。

1: Musubidachi
2: Musubidachi
3: Open both hands and stretch them along both thighs respectively.

▶ ジオン篇

観空(大)篇

〔特徴〕

　この形は四方、八方に敵を仮想して各方面からの様々な攻撃を捌き、受けて反撃するもので非常に変化に富んだ形である。技の緩急、力の強弱、体の伸縮はもちろん、転回、飛び上り、伏せなどがあり大変難しい形である。

KANKU(DAI)is a KATA requiring a variety of techniques in defense against opponents attacking from many directions and utilizes skillful counterattacks. It is an extremely difficult KATA using quick and slow techniques,strong and light power,and elastic body action suchas rotating, jumping, and dropping horizontally.

※従来の外受けを内受けに、内受けを外受けに統一した。
※Traditional Sotouke is changed into Uchiuke and Uchiuke is changed into Sotouke respectively.

KANKU(DAI)

直立　　　用意

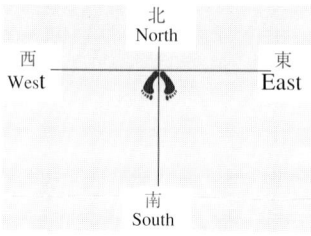

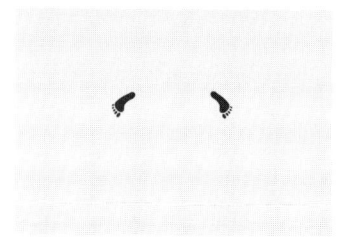

足の動作●結び立ち。
立ち方●結び立ち。
手の動作●両手は開いて大腿部両側に付けて伸ばす。

足の動作●結び立ちから八字立ち。
立ち方●八字立ち。
手の動作●静かにゆっくり両掌を右を上に斜めに重ねる。

着眼点●南

立ち方●❷のまま。
手の動作●両掌重ねたまま額斜め上に（❸は途中の姿勢止まらない）。

備考●ゆっくり。

着眼点●指の間から空を観る気持で（目の高さより手の動きに合わせる）。

Remarks
1: Feet
2: Stance
3: Hands
4: Point to see

1: Musubidachi.
2: Musubidachi.
3: Open both hands and stretch arms down to both sides of thighs.

1: From Musubidachi to Hachijidachi
2: Hachijidachi
3: Place both palms in front of the body with right palm on top.
4: South

2: Same as in ❷.
3: While placing right palm on left palm, lift them diagonally above forehead (❸ Shows form during the move. Do not stop at this point.).
4: As if looking up to the sky between fingers (follow your hands upward when they reach eye level).

Note: Do slowly.

観空（大）

1 挙動　　　　　　　　　　　　　　2 挙動

立ち方●❷のまま。
手の動作●両掌を左右に（速く）開き、止めずにゆっくりと下腹部前へ、両肘は軽く伸ばし静かに孤を描く。左掌を縦に（甲斜め左下向き）右掌は左掌の上に斜めに軽く重ねる（甲右下向き）（❺は途中の姿勢止まらない）。

備考●開くとき、とめない。

着眼点●南

2:Same as in ❷.
3:Spread both palms swiftly to each side, then, bring them down slowly without stopping to the front of lower abdomen. Stretch both elbows lightly and describe an arc slowly. Left palm is vertical, (with back of hand facing diagonally downward to the left).Right hand is placed lightly on left palm (back of hand facing downward to the right). (❺ Shows form during the move. Do not stop at this point.)
4:South
Note:Do not interrupt the motion after opening the arms.

3挙動　　4挙動

足の動作●八字立ち自然体より左足を東へすり出す。
立ち方●右後屈立ち。
手の動作●左背腕左側面上段受け（左甲後向き）。右掌胸前に構える（右甲下向き）。

留意点●❼—❽はサッと早く続ける（腕の動きより後屈立ちに注意）。

備考●後屈立ち、重心の割合は後足7、前足3のバランス。
着眼点●東

足の動作●方向を西へ変える。
立ち方●左後屈立ち。
手の動作●右背腕右側面上段受け（右甲後向き）、左掌胸前に構える（左甲下向き）。

着眼点●西

1: Slide left foot toward east (from Hachijidachi).
2: Right-Kokutsudachi
3: Left-Haiwan left side Jyodan-Uke (Back of left hand faces north) Hold open right hand in front of chest (Back of right hand faces downward)
4: East

Note: Motion ❼-❽ must be done quickly. Pay attention more to Kokutsudachi than arm movement.

1: Turn and face west.
2: Left-Kokutsudachi
3: Right-Haiwan right side Jyodan-Uke. (Back of right hand faces north) Hold left palm in front of chest. (Back of left hand faces downward)
4: West

観空（大）

5 挙動　　6 挙動　　7 挙動

⓾　　**⓫**　　**⓬**

足の動作●左後屈立ちより足の位置をそのまま膝を軽く伸ばす。
立ち方●八字立ち。
手の動作●左中段縦手刀受け。右拳右腰に引く（左掌は右肘下からゆっくり大きく）（❾は途中の姿勢止まらない）。

備考●ゆっくり。

着眼点●南

立ち方●⓾のまま。
手の動作●右中段突き。左拳左腰に引く。

着眼点●南

足の動作●八字立ち自然体より足の位置そのまま腰左転。
立ち方●左前屈。
手の動作●右中段外受け。左拳⓫のまま。

備考●前屈を正確に。両足が床面に密着すること（特に後足刀部）。

着眼点●南

1:Without changing location of feet, from Left-Kokutsudachi, stretch both knees lightly.
2:Hachijidachi
3:Left-Chudan-Tate-Shutouke. Pull down right fist to right hip (make a slow large movement of the open left hand from under neath the right elbow). (❾ Shows form during the move. Do not stop at this point.)
4:South

Note:Do slowly

2:Same as in ⓾.
3:Right-Chudantsuki. Pull back left fist to the left hip.
4:South

1:Twist hips to the left without changing location of feet.
2:Left-Zenkutsu
3:Right-Chudanuke. Left fist same as in ⓫.
4:South

Note:Do Zenkutsu accurately. Both foot must stick to the floor firmly (especially back foot edge).

▶観空（大）篇

8 挙動　　9 挙動　　10 挙動

【⓯を北から見る】
⓯seen from north.

8挙動

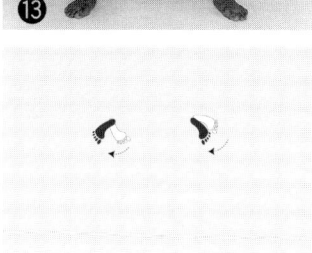

足の動作●左前屈を八字立ち自然体へもどす。
立ち方●八字立ち。
手の動作●左中段突き。右拳右腰に引く。

着眼点●南

1:Return to Hachijidachi from Left-Zenkutsudachi.
2:Hachijidachi
3:Left-Chudantsuki.Pull back right fist to the right hip.
4:South

9挙動

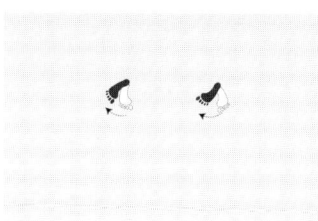

足の動作●八字立ち自然体より足の位置そのまま腰右転。
立ち方●右前屈。
手の動作●左中段外受け。右拳⓭のまま。

備考●⓬と同じく

着眼点●南

1:Twist hips to right without changing location of feet.
2:Right-Zenkutsu
3:Left-Chudan-Sotouke. Right fist same as in 13.
4:South

Note:Same as in ⓬.

10挙動

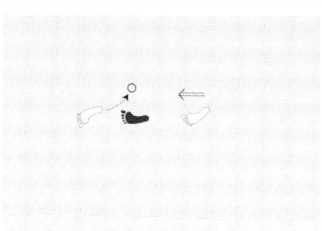

足の動作●右前屈より左足を半歩引き寄せ、左脚を軸として腰右転。右足裏を左膝横に添える。
立ち方●左脚立ち。
手の動作●両拳左腰構え。右拳（甲前向）を左拳の上（甲下向）に重ねる。

留意点●両拳左腰への引手が不充分な場合

着眼点●北

1:Pull left foot half step forward from Right-Zenkutsu and stand on the left foot, then, pivoting on left foot, turn hips to the right. Place right foot sole lightly on the left knee.
2:Standing on left foot.
3:Hold both fists on the left hip, with right fist (back of fist facing outside) on top of the left fist (back of fist facing downward)
4:North

Point:Pull back both fists to the left hip.

80

観空（大）

11挙動

⑰

⑱
【⑰を北から見る】
⑰seen from north.

足の動作●北へ右横蹴上げ。
立ち方●左脚立ち。
手の動作●右裏拳上段横回し打。左拳そのまま。

備考●蹴上げ（目標中段）。

着眼点●北

1: Right-Yokokeage toward north.
2: Standing on the left foot.
3: Jyodan-Yokomawashiuchi with Right-Uraken. Left fist same as in ⑮.
4: North

Note: Keage(Aiming at Chudan).

12挙動

⑲

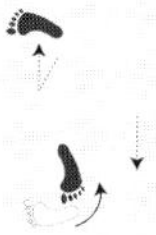

足の動作●右足を北におろす。
立ち方●右後屈立ち。
手の動作●左手刀中段受け。右手刀胸前。

着眼点●南

1: Put down right foot toward north.
2: Right-Kokutsudachi
3: Left-Shuto-Chudan-Uke. Hold Right-Shuto in front of the chest.
4: South

▶観空（大）篇　81

13挙動　　14挙動　　15挙動

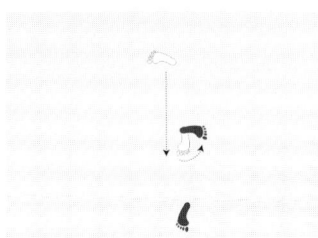

足の動作●右足南へ1歩進める。
立ち方●左後屈立ち。
手の動作●右手刀中段受け。左手刀胸前。

着眼点●南

足の動作●左足南へ1歩進める。
立ち方●右後屈立ち。
手の動作●左手刀中段受け。右手刀胸前。

着眼点●南

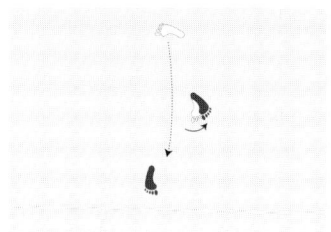

足の動作●右足南へ1歩進める。
立ち方●右前屈立ち。
手の動作●右中段4本貫手（甲右向き）。左掌中段押え受け（甲上向き）

留意点●①気合
②前屈立ちを正確に。足刀及び足裏を床面に密着させる。

備考●足刀及び足裏の床面に対する密着は全てに言える。

着眼点●南

1: Take right foot one step toward south.
2: Left-Kokutsudachi
3: Right-Shuto-Chudanuke. Hold Left-Shuto in front of the chest.
4: South

1: Take left foot one step toward south.
2: Right-Kokutsudachi
3: Left-Shuto-Chudan-Uke. Hold Right-Shuto in front of the chest.
4: South

1: Take right foot one step toward south.
2: Right-Zenkutsudachi
3: Right-Chudan-Shihon-Nukite. Left-Palm-Chudan-Osaeuke (back of hand facing upward).
4: South

Point: ①Kiai
②Zenkutsudachi must be done accurately. Contact Sokuto (edge of foot) and Ashiura (sole of foot) with floor firmly.
Note: This contacting the feet with the floor can be said to apply for every case.

観空（大）

16挙動

㉓　㉔【㉓を北から見る】㉓seen from north.　㉕【㉕を北から見る】㉖seen from north.

足の動作●右脚を軸に腰を左転し北へ向く。
立ち方●左前屈立ち（逆半身）。
手の動作●右手刀上段横回し打。左掌額前上段受け（㉓は途中の姿勢止まらない）。

着眼点●北

1:Pivoting on right foot, turn hips to the left, facing north.
2:Left-Zenkutsudachi (hips in reverse Hanmi)
3:Jyodan-Yokomawashiuchi with Right-Shuto. Left-palm-Jyodan-Uke in front of forehead. (㉓ Shows form during the move. Do not stop at this point.)
4:North

▶観空(大)篇　83

17挙動

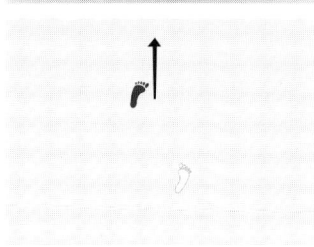

㉗

【㉗を北から見る】

㉗ seen from north

㉘

㉙

足の動作●右前蹴り。
立ち方●左脚立ち。
手の動作●上体㉕のまま。

着眼点●北

1:Right-Maegeri
2:Stand on the left foot.
3:Same as in ㉕.
4:North

18挙動

観空（大）
19挙動

㉚ ㉛

【㉚を西から見る】
㉚ seen from west.

㉜

足の動作●右足を北におろす。
立ち方●右後屈立ち。
手の動作●右拳右側面上段受け。左拳左側面下段受け（いったん右掌を左肘下から、左掌は右肩口から握りながら互いに引きしぼるように）（㉙は途中の姿勢止まらない）。

着眼点●南

足の動作●右脚を軸に、左足を前屈立ちに膝を屈する。
立ち方●左前屈立ち。
手の動作●右手刀下段打込み（甲下向き）。左掌上段流し受け（甲横向き）。

着眼点●南

1: While putting down right foot toward north, turn hips to left.
2: Right-Kokutsudachi
3: Right fist Right side Jyodan-Uke. Left fist Left side Gedan-Uke (gripping both fists, pull apart right fist from underneath left elbow and left fist from top of right shoulder). (㉙ Shows form during the move. Do not stop at this point.)
4: South

1: Pivoting on the right foot, bend left knee to Zenkutsudachi.
2: Left-Zenkutsudachi
3: Right-Shuto-Gedan-Uchikomi (back of hand facing downward). Left-palm-Jyodan-Nagashiuke above the right shoulder (back of hand facing outside).
4: South

▶観空（大）篇　85

20挙動

㉝

【㉝を北から見る】

㉝ seen from north

足の動作●左足を右足にすこし引き寄せる。
立ち方●左足前レの字立ち。
手の動作●左拳下段に伸ばす。右拳右腰に引く。

備考●ゆっくり

着眼点●南

1:Pull left foot to the right foot slightly.
2:Stand naturally, with left foot in front.
3:Stretch left fist downward. Pull back right fist to right hip.
4:South

Note:Do slowly.

21挙動

㉟

足の動作●右足そのままの位置で腰を左転。
立ち方●左前屈立ち（逆半身）。
手の動作●右手刀上段横回し打ち。左掌額前上段受け。

着眼点●南

1:Turn hips to left without changing location of right foot.
2:Left-Zenkutsudachi (hips in reverse Hanmi)
3:Jyodan-Yokomawashiuchi with Right-Shuto. Left-palm-Jyodan-Uke in front of forehead.
4:South

観空（大）

22挙動

㊱ ㊲ ㊳

【㊲を北から見る】

㊲ seen from north

足の動作●右前蹴り。
立ち方●左脚立ち。
手の動作●上体㉟のまま。

着眼点●南

1:Right-Maegeri
2:Stand on the left foot.
3:Same as in ㉟.
4:South

▶観空（大）篇

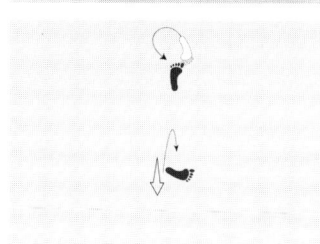

23挙動

㊴

㊵

【㊴を北から見る】

㊴ seen from north

足の動作●右足を南におろす。
立ち方●右後屈立ち。
手の動作●右拳右側面上段受け。左拳左側面下段受け（要領は㉚と同様）。

着眼点●北

1: Put down right foot toward south.
2: Right-Kokutsudachi
3: Right-fist-right-side-Jyodan-Uke. Left-fist-left-side-Gedan-Uke (Movement same as in ㉚).
4: North

24挙動

㊶

㊷

【㊶を北から見る】

㊶ seen from north

足の動作●右脚を軸に左脚を前屈立ちに膝を屈する。
立ち方●左前屈立ち。
手の動作●右手刀下段打込み（甲下向き）。左掌上段流し受け（甲横向き）。

着眼点●北

1: Pivoting on the right foot, bend left knee to Zenkutsudachi.
2: Left-Zenkutsudachi
3: Right-Shuto-Gedan-Uchikomi (back of hand facing downward). Left-palm-Jyodan-Nagashiuke above right shoulder (back of hand facing outside).
4: North

観空（大）

25挙動　　26挙動

❹❹ を北から見る】

❹❹ seen from north

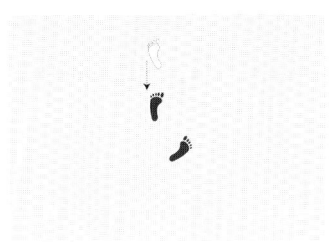

足の動作●左足を右足にすこし引き寄せる。
立ち方●左足前レの字立ち。
手の動作●左拳下段に伸ばす。右拳右腰に引く。

備考●ゆっくり

着眼点●北

足の動作●右脚を軸として腰を左転、左足裏を右膝横に添える。
立ち方●右脚立ち。
手の動作●両拳右腰構え。左拳（甲前向き）を右拳の上（甲下向き）に重ねる。

着眼点●西

1: Pull left foot to the right foot slightly.
2: Stand naturally with left foot in front.
3: Stretch left fist downward. Pull back right fist to the right hip.
4: North

Note: Do slowly

1: Pivoting on the right foot, turn the hips to left. Place left sole on the right knee.
2: Stand on right foot.
3: Hold both fists on the right hip with left fist (back of fist facing outside) on top of the right fist (back of fist facing downward).
4: West

▶観空(大)篇　89

27挙動

㊻

【㊻を北から見る】

㊻ seen from north

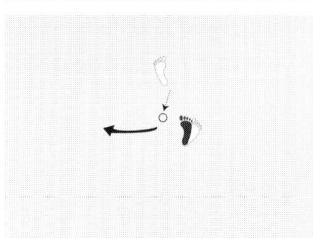

㊼

足の動作●西へ左横蹴上げ。
立ち方●右脚立ち。
手の動作●左裏拳上段横回し打ち。右拳㊹のまま。

備考●蹴上げ（目標中段）

留意点●横蹴りの場合、上体が力み過ぎて引手が横蹴りと同時に離れないこと。

着眼点●西

1: Left-Yokokeage toward west.
2: Stand on right foot.
3: Jyodan-Yokomawashiuchi with Left-Uraken. Right fist same as in ㊹.
4: West

Note: Keage (aiming at Chudan)

Point: In case of Yokogeri, too much tension of the upper body should be avoided and Hikite should not come apart when executing Yokogeri.

28挙動

㊽

【㊽を北から見る】

㊽ seen from north

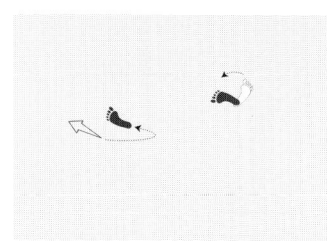

㊾

足の動作●左脚を西へおろし、腰を左転し左前屈立ちとなる。
立ち方●左前屈立ち。
手の動作●右前猿臂（左掌に当てる）。

備考●左腕平行。

着眼点●西

1: Put down left foot toward west and turn hips to the left to pose Left-Zenkutsudachi.
2: Left-Zenkutsudachi
3: Right-elbow-Enpi (hitting against the left palm)
4: West

Note: Left arm is parallel with floor.

観空（大）

29挙動

⑤⓪

【⑤⓪を北から見る】

⑤⓪ seen from north

足の動作●左脚を軸に腰を右転しながら右足裏を左膝横に添える。
立ち方●左脚立ち。
手の動作●両拳左腰構え。右拳（甲前向き）を左拳の上（甲下向き）に重ねる。

着眼点●東

1: Pivoting on the left foot, turn hips to the right. Place right sole on left knee.
2: Stand on left foot.
3: Hold both fists on the left hip with right fist (back of fist facing outside) on top of the left fist (back of fist facing downward).
4: East

30挙動

⑤②  ⑤③

【⑤②を北から見る】

⑤② seen from north

足の動作●東へ右横蹴上げ。
立ち方●左脚立ち。
手の動作●右裏拳上段横回し打ち。左拳⑤⓪のまま。

備考●蹴上げ（目標中段）。

着眼点●東

1: Right-Yokokeage toward east.
2: Stand on the left foot.
3: Jyodan-Yokomawashiuchi with Right-Uraken. Left fist same as in ⑤⓪.
4: East

Note: Keage(Aiming at Chudan).

31挙動

⑤④

【⑤④を北から見る】

❺④ seen from north

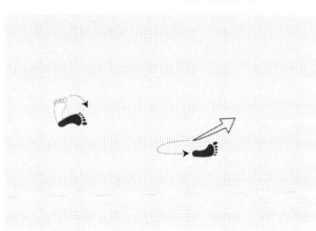

足の動作●右足を東へおろし、腰を右転し右前屈立ちとなる。
立ち方●右前屈立ち。
手の動作●左前猿臂（右掌に当てる）。

備考●右腕平行。

着眼点●東

1: Put down right foot toward east and turn hips to the right.
2: Right-Zenkutsudachi
3: Left-elbow-Empi (hitting against right palm).
4: East

Note: Right arm is parallel with floor.

32挙動

⑤⑥

【⑤⑥を北から見る】

❺⑥ seen from north

足の動作●右脚を軸にし、腰を左転。
立ち方●右後屈立ち。
手の動作●左手刀中段受け。右手刀胸前。

着眼点●西

1: Pivoting on right foot, turn hips to the left.
2: Right-Kokutsudachi
3: Left-Shuto-Chudanuke. Hold Right-Shuto in front of the chest.
4: West

観空（大）

33挙動

⑱

【⑱を北から見る】

⑲ seen from north

足の動作●左脚を軸に右足を北西に1歩進める。
立ち方●左後屈立ち。
手の動作●右手刀中段受け。左手刀胸前。

着眼点●北西

1:Pivoting on left foot, take right foot one step toward northwest.
2:Left-Kokutsudachi
3:Right-Shuto-Chudanuke.Hold Left-Shuto in front of the chest.
4:Northwest

34挙動

⑳

【⑳を北から見る】

㉑ seen from north

足の動作●左脚を軸に右足を東に1歩進める。
立ち方●左後屈立ち。
手の動作●右手刀中段受け。左手刀胸前。

着眼点●東

1:Pivoting on left foot, take right foot one step toward east.
2:Left-Kokutsudachi
3:Right-Shuto-Chudan-Uke.Hold Left-Shuto in front of the chest.
4:East

▶観空(大)篇 93

35挙動

⑥②

【⑥②を北から見る】
⑥② seen from north

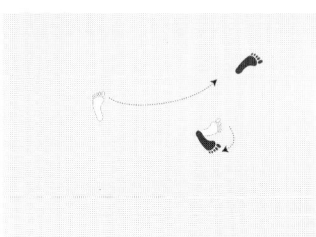

足の動作●右脚を軸に左足を
東北に1歩進める。
立ち方●右後屈立ち。
手の動作●左手刀中段受け。
右手刀胸前。

着眼点●北東

1:Pivoting on right foot, take left foot a step toward northeast.
2:Right-Kokutsudachi
3:Left-Shuto-Chudan-Uke. Hold Right-Shuto in front of the chest.
4:Northeast

36挙動

⑥④

【⑥④を北から見る】
⑥④ seen from north

足の動作●左足を北に移す。
立ち方●左前屈立ち（逆半身）。
手の動作●右手刀上段横回し
打ち。左掌額前上段受け。

着眼点●北

1:Bring left foot to north.
2:Left-Zenkutsudachi
3:Jyodan-Yokomawashiuchi (hips in reverse Hanmi) with Right-Shuto. Left-palm-Jyodan-Uke in front of forehead.
4:North

37挙動

⑯

⑰
【⑯を北から見る】

⑯ seen from north

⑱

⑲
【⑱を北から見る】

⑱ seen from north

足の動作●北へ右前蹴り。
立ち方●左脚立ち。
手の動作●手の位置は⑭のまま。

着眼点●北

1:Right-Maegeri toward north.
2:Stand on the left foot.
3:Hands position is same as in ⑭.
4:North

▶観空(大)篇 95

38挙動

⑦⓪

【⑦⓪を北から見る】

⑦⓪ seen from north

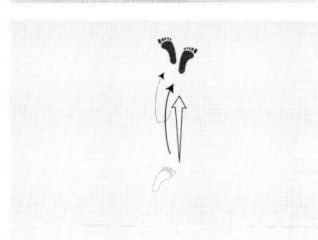

足の動作●右足から北へ大きく飛び込む。
立ち方●右脚前交差立ち（左足を右足後ろに交差）。
手の動作●右裏拳縦回し打ち。左拳左腰に引く（⑱は途中の姿勢止まらない）。

留意点●交差立ちは右足に左足を充分に引きつける。

着眼点●北

1: Take a long jumping step toward north, with right foot at first.
2: Kosadachi with right foot in front (left foot comes behind right ankle).
3: Right-Uraken-Tatemawashiuchi. Pull back left fist to the left hip. (⑱Shows form during the move. Do not stop at this point)
4: North

Point: At Kosadachi position, draw right foot to left foot closely.

39挙動

⑦② ⑦③

【⑦②を北から見る】

⑦② seen from north

足の動作●左足を南へ引く。
立ち方●右前屈立ち。（半身）
手の動作●右中段外受け。左拳左腰に引く。

着眼点●北

1: Pull back left foot toward south.
2: Right-Zenkutsudachi（hips in Hanmi position）
3: Right-Chudan-Uke. Hold left fist on the left hip.
4: North

観空（大）

40挙動

⑭

⑮

【⑭を北から見る】

⑭ seen from north

立ち方●⑫のまま。
手の動作●左中段逆突き。右拳右腰に引く。

着眼点●北

2:Same as in ⑫.
3:Left-Chudan-Gyakutsuki. Pull back right fist to the right hip.
4:North

41挙動

⑯

⑰

【⑯を北から見る】

⑯ seen from north

立ち方●⑫のまま。
手の動作●右中段順突き。左拳左腰に引く。

備考●⑭、⑯は連続で。

着眼点●北

2:Same as in ⑫.
3:Right-Chudan-Jyuntsuki. Pull back left fist to the left hip.
4:North

Note: ⑭ and ⑯ must be done in continuous movement.

42挙動

⑦⑧ ⑦⑨ ⑧⓪

足の動作●左脚を軸に腰左転、南へふり向き、右膝を高くかい込む。
立ち方●左脚立ち。
手の動作●右裏突き。左掌右手首横添え（両手を右大腿の両側からスリあげる）。

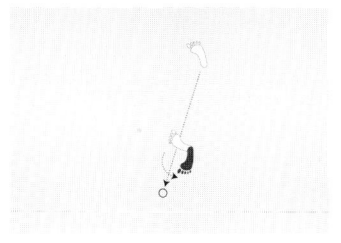

着眼点●南

1: Pivoting on the left foot, turn hips to the left, facing south, then, lift right knee up high.
2: Stand on the left foot
3: Right-Uratsuki. Scoop up hands from both sides of right thigh and place left palm on the right wrist.
4: South

留意点●両腕を右大腿の両側からすり上げる。このとき、右膝を高くかい込むこと。

Point: Both hands glide up from both sides of right thigh. At this time right knee is lifted high.

挙動の分解42
Kanku(Dai) Kumite in detail

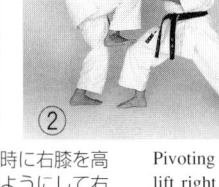

① ② ③

左脚を軸として左転、後方へふり向くと同時に右膝を高くあげ、両掌は右腿左右両側からすり出すようにして右拳（甲下）手首に左掌を添えて突き出す。あげた右膝頭と右手肘は拳1つくらいの間隔をとる。

Pivoting on the left foot, turn to the left. When body turns 180 degrees, lift right knee up high, and scoop up hands from both sides of right thigh, with left palm placed on the wrist of right hand (back of hand facing downward), and thrust them forward. Leave space about one fist between lifted right kneecap and right elbow.

観空（大）

43挙動　　　44挙動

【❽❷を北から見る】

❽❷ seen from north

足の動作●左脚を軸に右足を南へおろし、右膝を充分に屈し、体を地に伏せる。
立ち方●右足前伏せ（右前屈）。
手の動作●両掌肘立伏せ。
備考●4mぐらい前を見る。

足の動作●右脚を軸に腰左転、北へふり向く。
立ち方●右後屈立ち。
手の動作●左手刀下段受け（甲上向き）。右手刀胸前構え（甲下向き）。

※❽❶**留意点**●後足の足刀部が床面より浮いてはならない。床面に密着すること。

着眼点●南

1: Put down right foot toward south. Bend right knee deeply, then, drop to the body Fuse style.
2: Fuse with right foot in front. (Right-Zenkutsu)
3: Push up with both palms.
4: South
Note: Look at about 4m front.

着眼点●北

1: Pivoting on the right foot, turn hips to the left, facing north.
2: Right-Kokutsudachi
3: Left-Shuto-Gedan-Uke (back of hand facing upward). Hold Right-Shuto (back of hand facing downward) in front of the chest.
4: North

※❽❶**Point**: Don't lift edge of back foot from floor. Foot edge must stick to the floor.

挙動の分解43
Kanku(Dai)
Kumite in detail

右前屈、両掌は軽く地に着けて伏せる姿勢。ただし顔は4mぐらい前方を見つめる気持でややあげる。

Right-Zenkutsu, both palms are touched to the floor lightly in Fuse position. In this case face is lifted up a little looking at about 4m front.

▶観空（大）篇　99

45挙動

⑧④

⑧⑤

【⑧④を北から見る】

⑧④ seen from north

足の動作●右足を北へ1歩進める。
立ち方●左後屈立ち。
手の動作●右手刀中段受け。左手刀胸前。

着眼点●北

1:Take right foot one step toward north.
2:Left-Kokutsudachi
3:Right-Shuto-Chudan-Uke. Hold Left-Shuto in front of the chest.
4:North

46挙動

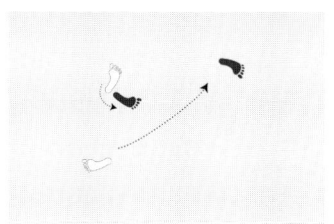

⑧⑥

足の動作●右脚を軸とし、腰を左転、左足を東に移動させる。
立ち方●左前屈立ち。（半身）
手の動作●左中段外受け。右拳右腰に引く。

着眼点●東

1:Pivoting on the right foot, turn hips to the left, bring left foot toward east.
2:Left-Zenkutsudachi（hips in Hanmi position）
3:Left-Chudan-Uke. Pull back right fist to the right hip.
4:East

観空（大）

47挙動　48挙動　49挙動

立ち方●⑧のまま。
手の動作●右中段逆突き。左拳左腰に引く。

着眼点●東

足の動作●左脚を軸に腰を右転、西を向く。
立ち方●右前屈立ち。（半身）
手の動作●右中段外受け。左拳右腰に引く。

着眼点●西

立ち方●⑧のまま。
手の動作●左中段逆突き。右拳右腰に引く。

着眼点●西

2:Same as in ⑧.
3:Right-Chudan-Gyakutsuki. Pull back left fist to the left hip.
4:East

1:Pivoting on the left foot, turn hips to the right, facing west.
2:Right-Zenkutsudachi（hips in Hanmi position）
3:Right-Chudan-Uke. Pull back left fist to the left hip.
4:West

2:Same as in ⑧.
3:Left-Chudan-Gyakutsuki. Pull back right fist to the right hip.
4:West

▶観空(大)篇　101

50挙動　51挙動

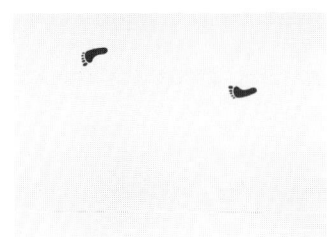

❾⓿　❾❶　❾❷

【❾❶を北から見る】

❾❶ seen from north

立ち方●❽❽のまま。
手の動作●右中段順突き。左拳左腰に引く。

備考●❽❾❾⓿は連続で。

着眼点●西

足の動作●左脚を軸に右脚裏を左膝横に添える。
立ち方●左脚立ち。
手の動作●両拳左腰構え左脚立ち。右拳を（甲前向き）左拳の上（甲下向き）に重ねる。

着眼点●北

2:Same as in ❽❽.
3:Right-Chudan-Juntsuki. Pull back left fist to the left hip.
4:West

Note: ❽❾ and ❾⓿ must be done in continuous movement.

1:Pivoting on the left foot lift right foot up to side of left knee.
2:Stand on left foot.
3:Hold both fists on the left hip with right fist (back of hand facing outside) on top of the left fist (back of hand facing downward)
4:North

102

52挙動

⑨③

⑨④

【⑨③を北から見る】

⑨③ seen from north

足の動作●北へ右横蹴上げ。
立ち方●⑨①のまま。
手の動作●右裏拳上段横回し打ち。

備考●蹴上げ（目標中段）。

着眼点●北

1:Right-Yokokeage toward north.
2:Stand on the left foot. Same as in ⑨①.
3:Jyodan -Yokomawashiuchi with Right-Uraken.
4:North

Note:Keage(Aiming at Chudan).

観空（大）
53挙動

⑨⑤

足の動作●右足を北におろす。
立ち方●右後屈立ち。
手の動作●左手刀中段受け。
右手刀胸前。

着眼点●南

1:Put down right foot toward north.
2:Right-Kokutsudachi
3:Left-Shuto-Chudan-Uke. Hold Right-Shuto in front of the chest.
4:South

54挙動

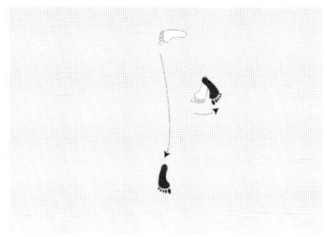

足の動作●右足を南へ１歩進める。
立ち方●右前屈立ち。
手の動作●右中段四本貫手（甲右向き）。左掌押え受け（右肘下）。

着眼点●南

1:Take right foot one step toward south.
2:Right-Zenkutsudachi
3:Right-Chudan-Shihon-Nukite. Left-palm-Osaeuke under the right elbow (back of right hand faces right).
4:South

⑨⑨
1:Pivoting on the right foot, turn hips to the left with a big motion, then, step left foot toward south to make feet parallel.
2:Kibadachi
3:Left-Uraken-Jyodan-Tatemawashi uke. Pull back right fist to the right hip (twist right wrist to the right, and with right palm as the center axis, turn while twisting upper body).
4:South

104

観空（大）

55挙動　　56挙動　　57挙動

足の動作●右脚を軸に腰を大きく左転させ、左足を南に進め、右足、左足を一線上に置く。
立ち方●騎馬立ち。
手の動作●左裏拳上段縦回し打ち。右拳右腰（右掌手首を右にひねり、右掌を中心に上体をひねりながら回す）。

着眼点●南

足の動作●南へ寄り足。
立ち方●騎馬立ち。
手の動作●左拳槌中段横打ち（いったん左拳を右肩口にとってから）。右拳右腰に引く。

着眼点●南

1: Yoriashi (slide) toward south.
2: Kibadachi
3: Left-Kentsui-Chudan-Yokouchi (strike after pulling back left fist to the right shoulder). Hold right fist on the right hip.
4: South

足の動作●⑩のまま。
立ち方●⑩のまま。
手の動作●右前猿臂（左掌に当てる）。

着眼点●南

1: Kibadachi
2: Kibadachi
3: Right-elbow-Enpi (hitting against left palm)
4: South

拳動の分解55　Kanku(Dai) Kumite in detail

右手を右回しに逆にひねられたとき、上体を前に出しながら右手を右肩の上に、体と共に肘を中心にひねり回しながら、右脚を軸にして左回りに左足を前方に移す。

When right hand is twisted to right by opponent, thrust upper body forward, with right hand on right shoulder, then, twist body with elbows and pivoting on right foot, swing left foot toward front.

▶観空（大）篇　105

58挙動　　　　59挙動

【⑩を北から見る】

⑩ seen from north

足の動作●⑩のまま。
立ち方●⑩のまま。
手の動作●両拳左腰構え右拳（甲前向き）を左拳の上（甲下向き）に重ねる。

着眼点●北

足の動作●⑩のまま。
立ち方●⑩のまま。
手の動作●右下段払い。左拳左腰に引く。

着眼点●北

1:Same as in ⑩.
2:Kibadachi
3:Hold both fists on the left hip with right fist (back of hand facing outside) on top of the left fist (back of hand facing downward).
4:North

1:Same as in ⑩.
2:Kibadachi
3:Right-Gedanbarai. Hold left fist on the left hip.
4:North

観空（大）

60挙動

⑩⑤

【⑩⑤を北から見る】

⑩⑤ seen from north

⑩⑥

⑩⑦

⑩⑧

【⑩⑦を北から見る】

⑩⑦ seen from north

留意点●左拳は小指側で下段受け。左足は敏速に行う。

足の動作●右脚を軸に腰を大きく右転、左膝はすばやく北へ踏み込む。
立ち方●騎馬立ち。
手の動作●左拳下段受け（甲後向き）。右拳ふりあげ（甲後向き）左拳は大きく頭上から回しながら振りおろし、同時に右拳は頭上へ振りあげる（⑩⑤は途中の姿勢止まらない）。

着眼点●東

1: Pivoting on the right foot, turn hips to right with a big motion, and lift left knee high, then, stamp down left foot toward north.
2: Kibadachi
3: Left-Gedan-Uke (back of hand facing backward). Swing right fist above head (back of hand facing backward) while swinging down left fist from above head in a large arcline motion. (⑩⑤ Shows form during the move. Do not stop at this point.)
4: East

Point: Left fist Gedan-Uke is executed at little finger side of the left fist. Left foot must move quickly.

**挙動の分解60
Kanku(Dai)
Kumite in detail**

⑩

⑪

相手の中段右前蹴りに対し、頭上より、すばやく足首を流すように下段受けし、縦拳（落し突き）にして突く（右拳甲外）。

Against Chyudan-Right-Maegeri by opponent, Gedan-Uke by drifting down the ankle and thrust Tatekentsuki(Otoshitsuki)(back of right hand faces outward).

▶観空(大)篇　107

61挙動

【⑩を北から見る】

⑩ seen from north

足の動作●⑩のまま。
立ち方●⑩のまま。
手の動作●右拳落し突き。左拳はそのまま（右拳を左拳の後ろに手首が交差するように）。（左手首が上になる）、右拳甲外。

着眼点●東

1:same as in ⑩ .
2:Kibadachi.
3:Right fist Otoshitsuki.Left fist same as in 60. Cross both hands,with left wrist on top of right wrist and back of right fist faces outside.
4:East

62挙動

足の動作●両足を同時に引き寄せ、膝を伸ばして八字立ち。
立ち方●八字立ち。
手の動作●両掌上段交差受け。

留意点●交差受けは少し肘を曲げるぐらいで良い。勢いがついている箇所なので膝を強く伸ばしたり、踵を上げたりしないこと。

着眼点●東

1:Pulling both feet together at once, stretch knees.
2:Hachijidachi
3:Kosauke with both palms above head
4:East

Point:Kosauke should be done with a little bending of both elbows. As it is a powerful move, knees must not be overly straightened nor heels be lifted.

観空（大）

63挙動

⑫ ⑬ ⑭

【⑬を北から見る】

⑬ seen from north

足の動作●右脚を軸に腰を大きく右転。左足を南へ移す。
立ち方●右前屈立ち。
手の動作●両拳胸前交差、両掌は交差したまま握りしめながら胸前におろす。

備考●ゆっくり。

着眼点●北

1: Pivoting on the right foot, turn hips to right with a big motion, then, bring left foot to south.
2: Right-Zenkutsudachi
3: Ryoken-Munemae-Kosa, clench both hands above head, while crossing, then, pull down in front of the chest.
4: North

Note: Do slowly

挙動の分解62、63　Kanku(Dai) Kumite in detail

⑫ ⑬ ⑭

上段交叉受けをした後、両掌を中心に体を右に回し相手の手首をつかんで両手をさげ、右肩で相手の逆をとる。

After blocking with Jyodan-Kosauke, turn body to right with both palms on the center line. Pull down hands, while grabbing opponent's right wrist, then, apply "Gyaku" to his upper arm with right shoulder.

64挙動

足の動作●北へ二段蹴りをする。

立ち方●両足空中。

手の動作●二段蹴りをしながら右拳は胸前から頭上に振りかぶり、左拳は胸前へ軽く伸ばす。

留意点●気合。

着眼点●北

1:Execute Nidangeri toward north.
2:Both foot in the air.
3:While executing Nidangeri, swing right fist from chest to above head and stretch left fist lightly in front of the chest.
4:North

Point:Kiai

65挙動

⑫⓪

【⑫⓪を北から見る】

⑫⓪ seen from north

⑫① ⑫② ⑫③

足の動作●両足（右足前に）着地させる。
立ち方●右前屈立ち。
手の動作●右裏拳縦回し打ち。左拳左腰に引く。

留意点●右前屈立と右裏拳縦回し打ちは同時に決まるように。

着眼点●北

足の動作●右脚を軸に体を右回り、左足を東へ移し八字立ちとなる。
立ち方●八字立ち。
手の動作●右腕で下段を内から払うように回しながら左右両拳を大きく円を描いて回し、内側に交差しながら静かにおろし自然体にもどる（⑫③の姿勢は止めないで自然にもどす）。

備考●ゆっくり。

着眼点●南

1: Land with both feet (right foot in front).
2: Right-Zenkutsudachi
3: Right-Uraken-Tatemawashiuchi. Pull back left fist to the left hip.
4: North

Point: Right-Zenkutsudachi and Right-Uraken-Tatemawashiuchi should be performed at the same time.

1: Pivoting on the right foot, turn body to the right, then, Hachijidachi by bringing left foot toward east.
2: Hachijidachi
3: Turn right arm from Gedan in a sweeping motion from inside, draw a large circle with both fists, then, after crossing inward, drop hands slowly and returning to the original position. (⑫③ Shows form during the move. Do not stop at this point, return naturally to the standing Yame position.)
4: South
Note: Do slowly.

止め　　　　　直立

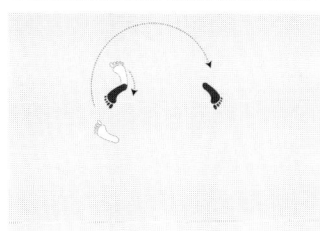

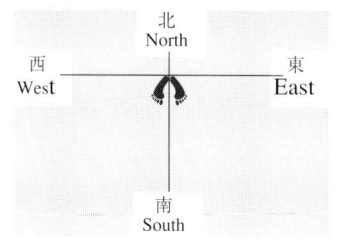

⑭　　　　　　⑮

備考●止めの時残心に、心がける。

Note: At Yame position, a state of alertness is important.

足の動作●結び立ち。
立ち方●結び立ち。
手の動作●両手は開いて大腿部両側に付けて伸ばす。

着眼点●南

1: Musubidachi.
2: Musubidachi.
3: Open both hands and stretch arms and fingers on both sides of the things.
4: South

セイエンチン篇

〔特徴〕

　セイエンチンは那覇手の系統の形であり、接近戦法が多く組み合わされ、蹴り技がなく、重厚な動きに特徴がある。
　演武線は左右対をなし、同一の動作が多く、呼吸と動作の緩急が一致している。

SEIENCHIN is a part of Naha-Te Schools, featured of its solid movement in well-combined infighting tactics without Keriwaza.
ENBUSEN is paired with right and left, performs same movements often and lenience and severity are harmonized in respiration and movements.

※従来の中段横受けを、中段外受けに、中段横打ち受けを、中段内受けに統一した。
※Traditional Chudan Yokouke is changed into Chudan Sotouke and Chudan Yokouchiuke is changed into Chudan Uchiuke respectively.

SEIENCHIN

直立　　用意1　　用意2　　1挙動

北 North
西 West — 東 East
南 South

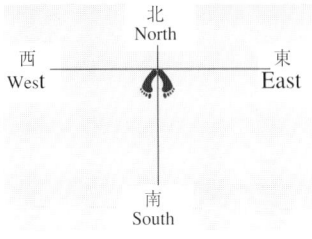

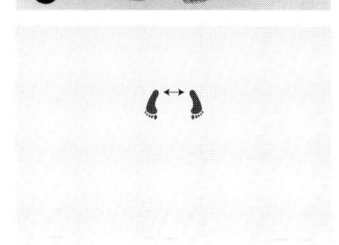

足の動作●爪先を開き、両踵をつける。
立ち方●結び立ち。
手の動作●両手は開き、体の両側に伸ばす。

着眼点●南

Remarks
1:Feet
2:Stance
3:Hands
4:Point to see

1:Put heels together with toes apart.
2:Musubidachi
3:Open hands and place them on both sides of the body, with arms and fingers straight down.
4:South

足の動作●❶のまま。
立ち方●結び立ち。
手の動作●両手は開き、左掌に右甲を重ね、ゆっくりと右甲を下に左掌を軽く押すようにして下腹部前に構える

着眼点●南

1:Same as ❶.
2:Musubidachi
3:Hold open hands in front of abdomen, with left hand on top.
4:South

足の動作●両足の爪先を軸にして両足踵を爪先の間隔に開き両足を平行にする。
立ち方●平行立ち。
手の動作●左右の手は握って体側に開き、下にさげ、肩を十分さげて臍下丹田に力を入れる。

着眼点●南

1:Pivoting on the tips of toes, move both heels until parallel.
2:Heikodachi
3:Gripping hands and stretch them down along side of the body. Pull down shoulders deeply and concentrate power in abdomen.
4:South

セイエンチン

2 挙動　　　3 挙動　　　4 挙動

❺

❻

❼

足の動作●右足を南西へ1歩円を描きながら踏み出す。
立ち方●四股立ち。
手の動作●両手は開いて甲を外に向け、両体側に自然に伸ばす。

着眼点●南

足の動作●❺のまま。
立ち方●四股立ち。
手の動作●左右の手を掬うようにしてゆっくりとあげ、胸の前で両手の甲を合わせる。

留意点●❺～❻への動作で肘の狭まりと手の掬い上げは連動すること。両手をあげるとき、肩をあげぬこと。両手と胸との間は、拳一握り分あける。

着眼点●南

足の動作●❺のまま。
立ち方●四股立ち。
手の動作●両手を握りながら体の両側へ引っ張るようにゆっくりと下段払いを行う。

留意点●❻～❼への下段払いが掻き分けにならないように。

着眼点●南

1:Take right foot one step toward southwest as if drawing a circle.
2:Shikodachi
3:Open both hands, back of hands facing outside, and stretch them naturally along side of the body.
4:South

1:Same as in ❺.
2:Shikodachi
3:Pull up both hands slowly as if scooping, then, put both back of hands together in front of the chest.
4:South

Point: While acting from ❺ to ❻ squeezing elbows and scooping up of hands must be done simultaneously. There should be fist space between both hands and breast.

1:Same as in ❺.
2:Shikodachi
3:Gripping gradually both hands, pull them away from each other slowly down along side of the body and execute Gedanbarai.
4:South

Point: Gedanbarai from ❻ to ❼ must not be Kakiwake.

▶セイエンチン篇　115

5挙動　　　6挙動　　　7挙動

⑧　　⑨　　⑩

足の動作●⑤のまま。
立ち方●四股立ち。
手の動作●両手は開いて南へ中段外受け、左は甲を下にして水月前に構える。

留意点●中段外受けは正面（南）に対して行う。

着眼点●南

1: Same as in ⑤.
2: Shikodachi
3: Open both hands, execute Chudan-Sotouke toward south with right palm, back of hand facing downward, and hold left palm, back of hand facing downward, in front of abdomen.
4: South

Point: Execute Chudan-Sotouke toward south.

足の動作●⑤のまま。
立ち方●四股立ち。
手の動作●右手を返して掛手を行う。

留意点●⑧⑨の手の動作は連続する。右中段外受けからの掛け手は素早くする。肘・手が上下前後に動くのは不可。

着眼点●南

1: Same as in ⑤.
2: Shikodachi
3: Turn around right hand, back of hand facing upward, and execute Kaketeuke.
4: South

Point: Hands in ⑧ and ⑨ must be a continuous movement. Kakete from Right-Chudan-Sotouke must act quickly. Elbows and hands must not move up and down or front and back.

足の動作●⑤のまま。
立ち方●四股立ち。
手の動作●掛けた右手を右脇へ引きながら左四本貫手にて南西方向へ突く。

留意点●動作はゆっくりと行う。引く右手は肘をさげるようにして肩をぜったいにあげぬこと。左貫手の方向は体面に沿って右肘下の方向に突く。

着眼点●南

1: Same as in ⑤.
2: Shikodachi
3: While pulling back right hand, used for Kaketeuke, to right side of the body, execute left hand strike toward southwest with Left-Nukite.
4: South

Point: Movements must be acted slowly. Keep right elbow low, when pulling back hand. Never raise right shoulder under any circumstances. The direction of Left-Nukite comes down toward right elbow closely along the body.

8挙動　　9挙動　　10挙動　　セイエンチン

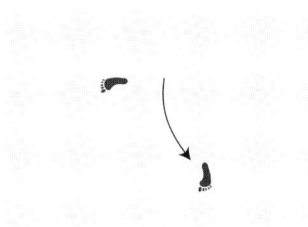

⑪　　⑫　　⑬

9挙動
足の動作●⑪のまま。
立ち方●四股立ち。
手の動作●左右の手を掬うようにしてゆっくりとあげ、両手の甲を胸の前で合わせる。

着眼点●南

10挙動
足の動作●⑪のまま。
立ち方●四股立ち。
手の動作●両手を握りながら体の両側へ引っ張るようにゆっくりと下段払いをする。

着眼点●南

8挙動
足の動作●左足を南東へ円を描くようにして前へ出す。
立ち方●四股立ち。
手の動作●両手は開いて体の両側に自然に伸ばす。

留意点●前進の運足は柔らかい円運動で進める。

着眼点●南

1: Same as in ⑪.
2: Shikodachi
3: Lift up both hands slowly as if scooping, then, put both back of hands together in front of the chest.
4: South

1: Same as in ⑪.
2: Shikodachi
3: Gripping gradually both hands, pull them away from each other slowly down alongside of the body and execute Gedanbarai.
4: South

1: Step left foot forward to southeast as if drawing a circle.
2: Shikodachi
3: Open both hands and stretch them naturally along side of the body.
4: South

Point: Stepping forward should be moved gently as if drawing a circle.

挙動の分解 2〜19　Seienchin Kumite in detail

構え姿勢。

① Kamae posture

中段突きを、左手下段払い。

② Withdrawing body toward right diagonally against oppnent's Right-Chudantsuki, execute Gedanbarai with left fist.

▶セイエンチン篇　117

11挙動　12挙動　13挙動

⑭　⑮　⑯

足の動作●⓫のまま。
立ち方●四股立ち。
手の動作●両拳を開いて左中段外受け、右手は水月前に構える。

着眼点●南

1: Same as in ⓫.
2: Shikodachi
3: Open both hands, execute Left-Chudan-Sotouke, and hold right palm in front of abdomen.
4: South

足の動作●⓫のまま。
立ち方●四股立ち。
手の動作●左手を返して掛け手を行う。

着眼点●南

1: Same as in ⓫.
2: Shikodachi
3: Turn around left hand and execute Kakete.
4: South

足の動作●⓫のまま。
立ち方●四股立ち。
手の動作●左手は左脇へ引きつけながら右四本貫手で南東方向へ突く。

着眼点●南

1: Same as in ⓫.
2: Shikodachi
3: While pulling back left hand to left side of the body, execute right hand strike toward southeast with Right-Yonhon-Nukite.
4: South

中段逆突きを、四股立ちになり、中段外受け。

③ Block opponent's Left-Chudan-Gyakutsuki with Chudan-Sotouke at Shikodachi by drawing back left foot.

掌をかえして相手の腕を捕る。

④ Turn round left palm and grab opponent's left arm.

腕を左脇へ引きつけて、脇腹を右拳で裏突きする。

⑤ Pull opponent's left arm toward left side of body, then, execute Uratsuki to his left side of body with right fist.

14挙動　15挙動　16挙動　セイエンチン

⑰　**⑱**　**⑲**

足の動作●右足を南西へ円を描きながら1歩進める。
立ち方●四股立ち。
手の動作●両手は開いて、体側へ自然に伸ばす。

着眼点●南

1: Step right foot forward to southwest as if drawing a circle.
2: Shikodachi
3: Open both hands, stretch them naturally along side of the body.
4: South

足の動作●⑰のまま。
立ち方●四股立ち。
手の動作●左右の手を掬うようにゆっくりあげ、胸の前で両手の甲を合わせる。

着眼点●南

1: Same as in ⑰.
2: Shikodachi
3: Pull up both hands slowly as if scooping, then, put both back of hands together in front of the chest.
4: South

足の動作●⑰のまま。
立ち方●四股立ち。
手の動作●両手を握りながら左右に引っ張るようにしてゆっくり下段払いを行う。

着眼点●南

1: Same as in ⑰.
2: Shikodachi
3: Gripping both hands, pull them away from each other slowly down along side of the body and execute Gedanbarai.
4: South

▶セイエンチン篇　119

17挙動　　18挙動　　19挙動

⑳

㉑

㉒

足の動作●⓱のまま。
立ち方●四股立ち。
手の動作●両手は開き右中段外受け、左手は水月前に構える。

着眼点●南

足の動作●⓱のまま。
立ち方●四股立ち。
手の動作●右手は返して掛け手をする。

着眼点●南

足の動作●⓱のまま。
立ち方●四股立ち。
手の動作●右手は右脇へゆっくり引きながら左四本貫手で南西方向を突く。

着眼点●南

1:Same as in ⓱.
2:Shikodachi
3:Open both hands, execute Right-Chudan-Sotouke, and hold left palm, back of hand facing downward in front of abdomen.
4:South

1:Same as in ⓱.
2:Shikodachi
3:Turn around right hand, and execute Kaketeuke.
4:South

1:Same as in ⓱.
2:Shikodachi
3:While pulling back right hand slowly to right side of body, execute left hand strike toward southwest with Yonhon-Nukite.
4:South

セイエンチン

20挙動

㉓

【㉓を西から見る】
㉔ ㉓ seen from west.

足の動作●左足に右足を引きつけて片足で立つ。
立ち方●
手の動作●左手は開いて掌を上にして水月前に引き、左掌の上に右拳の甲を下にして乗せる。
留意点●㉒〜㉓への移りで「足の動作」の立ちと、左右の手は連動すること。ただし、左右の手は自然に水月前に構える。
着眼点●南

1: Pull right foot to left foot and stand on left foot.
2: Stand on left foot.
3: Pull back left hand in front of abdomen, with palm facing upward, then, place right fist, back of hand facing downward on top of left palm.
4: South
Point: While moving from ㉒ to ㉓ standing on foot in Action of Foot and both hands should be moved simultaneously. In this case hold both hands in front of abdomen.

21挙動

㉕

【㉕を西から見る】
㉖ ㉕ seen from west.

足の動作●右足を前(南)へ踏み込み、左足を寄せる。
立ち方●右基立ち。
手の動作●右拳および左手を返して南へ押し込むように突く。
着眼点●南

1: Step right foot forward (toward south) and draw up left foot.
2: Right-Motodachi
3: While turning around right fist and left plam, strike them forward to south as if pushing.
4: South

挙動の分解20〜23　Seienchin Kumite in detail

⑥ 襟(えり)を捕ってきたとき。
Being grabbed by the collar from front.

⑦ 左手を開いて水月前に置き。 
Open left hand, place it in front of abdomen, then, put right fist, back of hand facing downward on top of left palm.

⑧ 右拳および左掌をかえして、相手の中心に向かって押し込む。
Turn around right fist and left palm, then, press them against center part of opponent.

▶セイエンチン篇　121

22挙動

㉗

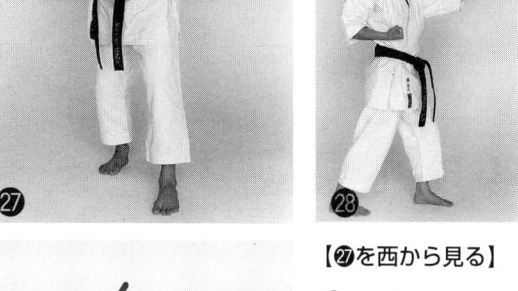

㉘

【㉗を西から見る】
㉗ seen from west.

足の動作●右足を後方へ1歩引く。
立ち方●左基立ち。
手の動作●右拳は脇へ引き、左手は掌を内に向けて左体側へ伸ばす。

着眼点●南

1: Pull right foot one step backward.
2: Left-Motodachi
3: Pull back right fist to right side of the body and stretch left hand straight along left side of the body, with palm facing inside.
4: South

23挙動

㉙

㉚

【㉙を西から見る】
㉙ seen from west.

足の動作●㉗のまま
立ち方●左基立ち。
手の動作●左手を中に入れ掌に対し右中段肘当てを行う。

留意点●肘当てのとき、腰を入れる。肘当が高くならぬよう留意すること。体の中央部に肘当てを行う。

着眼点●南

1: Same as in ㉒.
2: Left-Motodachi
3: Pull left hand inside and execute Right-Chudan elbow attack against left palm.
4: South
Point: When executing elbow attack, move right hip in. Pay attention that Hijiate is not executed to upper but centre part of the body.

両手を突き離すと同時に右足を踏み込む。 
⑨
While pushing him away with both hands, step right foot in.

中段突きしてくるのを、前足を引いて左小手で受ける。 
⑩
When opponent comes back with Chudantsuki, withdraw front foot and block with left Kote.

腕を捕って引き寄せ、右肘当て。 
⑪
Grabbing his right arm with blocking left hand and pulling him together, strike toward his Chudan with right elbow.

122

セイエンチン

24挙動　　　　　　25挙動　　　　　　26挙動

③を北西から見る】
③ seen from northwest.

足の動作●左足を軸にして右足を南西へ円を描きながら運ぶ。
立ち方●右三戦立ち。
手の動作●左手は開いて右拳拳槌部に添えて右手で中段外受けを行う。（拳支え受け）

着眼点●南西

1: Pivoting on the left foot, bring right foot to southwest as if drawing a circle.
2: Right-Sanchindachi
3: Put left hand beside Right-Kentsui and execute Chudan-Sotouke. (Ken-Sasaeuke).
4: Southwest

足の動作●左足を南西方向へ1歩踏み出す。
立ち方●四股立ち。
手の動作●左拳槌で下段へ打ち込み、右拳は脇へ引く。

着眼点●南西

1: Take left foot one step toward southwest.
2: Shikodachi
3: Execute Left-Kentsui toward Gedan(lower) and pull back the right fist to the side of body.
4: Southwest

足の動作●左足を後方へ1歩引く。
立ち方●四股立ち。
手の動作●右下段払いを行い左拳は脇へ引く。

留意点●最短距離で左拳打込みが極ったら、直ぐに左足を引いて四股立ち、右下段払いを行う。左拳・右拳の大振り・腰の上下は不可。

着眼点●南西

1: Pull left foot one step backward.
2: Shikodachi
3: Execute Right-Gedanbarai with right fist and pull back left fist to left side of body.
4: Southwest

Point: Immediately after finishing straight Ken-Uchi with left fist, Shikodachi by pulling back left foot and execute Right-Gedanbarai. Don't overswing right and left fist and also don't move too much up and down of the hips.

挙動の分解24〜29　Seienchin Kumite in detail

中段突きを、右中段拳支え受け。

⑫ Block opponent's Right-Chudan-tsuki with Right-Chudan-Ken-Sasasaeuke, while drawing front foot toward left diagonally.

手首を捕ると同時に、四股立ちとなり、左拳槌で急所に当てる。

⑬ While taking his right wrist with right hand, step left foot in to become Shikodachi, then, strike his groin with Left-Kentsui.

▶セイエンチン篇　123

27挙動　　　　28挙動　　　　29挙動

足の動作●右足を軸にして左足で円を描くようにして南東方向へ左足を1歩運ぶ。
立ち方●左三戦立ち。
手の動作●右手は開いて左拳槌部に添えて中段外受けを行う。(拳支え受け)

着眼点●南東

1:Pivoting on the right foot, take left foot a step toward southeast as if drawing a circle.
2:Left-Sanchindachi
3:Opening right hand, put it beside Left-Kentsui and execute Chudan-Uke. (Ken-Sasaeuke)

足の動作●前(左)足を軸にして南東方向へ右足を1歩踏み出す。
立ち方●四股立ち。
手の動作●右拳槌で下段へ打ち込み左拳は脇へ引く。

着眼点●南東

1:Pivoting on the front (left) foot, take right foot one step toward southeast and lower hips.
2:Shikodachi
3:Strike toward lower by right Kentsui, pull back left fist to side of the body.
4:Southeast

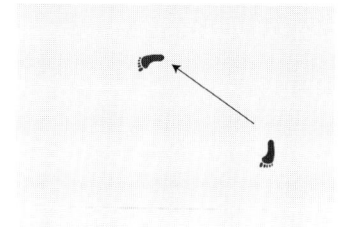

足の動作●右足を後方へ1歩引く。
立ち方●四股立ち。
手の動作●左下段払い、右拳は左脇へ引く。

着眼点●南東

1:Pull right foot one step backward.
2:Shikodachi
3:Execute Gedanbarai with left fist and pull back right fist to right side of the body.
4:Southeast

左手を首にかけ。 
⑭ After striking, bring up left hand and put it on his neck.

左手を後方へ大きく振る。 
⑮ Swing left hand backward.

相手を後方へ投げる。 
⑯ Throw down opponent backward.

突く。 
⑰ Lower hips and finish with Tsuki.

セイエンチン

30挙動　　　31挙動

㊳
㊴ 【㊳を東から見る】 
㊳ seen from east.
㊵
㊶ 【㊵を西から見る】 
㊵ seen from west.

足の動作●後（右）足を軸にして左足を北方向直線上に引く。
立ち方●四股立ち。
手の動作●両拳を開いて体の前面で交差させながら左手は額の前へ、右手は掌底で下へ押さえるようにゆっくり下段受けする。
留意点●手・足・腰は連動。（足が完全に極まって上段・下段の手だけが動かないこと）

着眼点●南

1: Pivoting on the hind (right) foot, pull back left foot toward north on a straight line with right foot.
2: Shikodachi
3: Opening fists, cross them in front of the body, then, bring left hand in front of forehead, while executing Gedan-Uke slowly with right hand as if pushing downward with Shotei.
4: South
Point: Actions of hands, feet and hips are in a linked manner. (When feet actions are finished, don't move hands only at Jyodan and/or Gedan).

足の動作●前（右）足を後方（北）直線上1歩引く。
立ち方●四股立ち。
手の動作●両手を体の前で交差しながらゆっくりと、左手は掌底で下段を押さえ右手は掌を外に向けて額の前に引く。
留意点●手・足・腰は連動。（㊳に同じ）
着眼点●南

1: Pull front (right) foot one step backward (toward north) on a straight line with left foot.
2: Shikodachi
3: After crossing both hands in front of body, control Gedan slowly with Left-Shotei and pull right hand upward in front of forehead, with palm facing outside.
4: South
Point: Hands, feet and hips should move in a linked manner. Same as in ㊳

挙動の分解30、31　Seienchin Kumite in detail

中段蹴りを、右手で掬いあげて捕る。 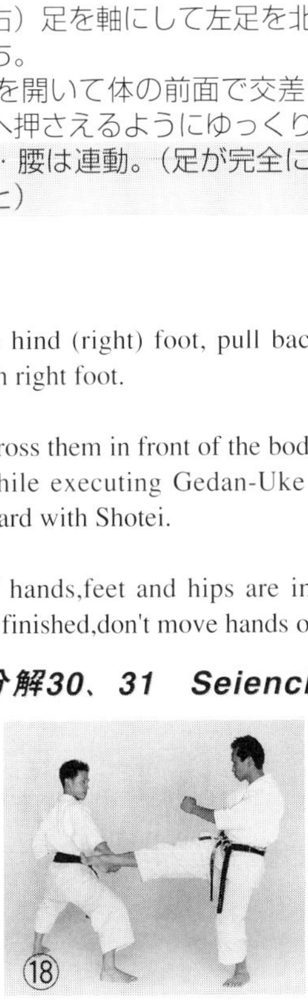
⑱ When opponent attacks with Chudangeri, grab his right foot with right hand as if scooping.

上段突きを揚げ受けし、腕を捕り。 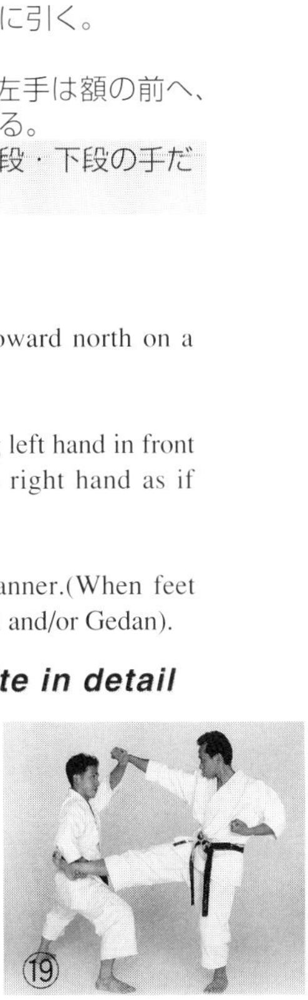
⑲ When he attacks further with Jyodantsuki, grab his right wrist with left hand.

左足で金的を蹴る。 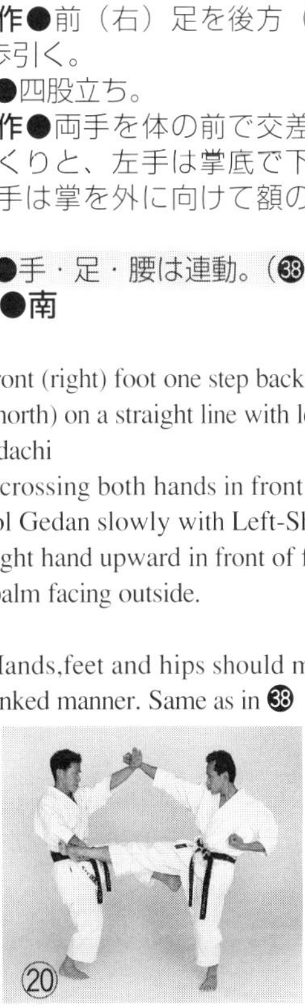
⑳ Finish by kicking Kinteki (groin) with left foot.

32挙動   33挙動

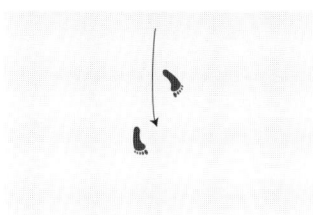

㊷   ㊸   ㊹   ㊺

【㊷を東から見る】
㊷ seen from east.

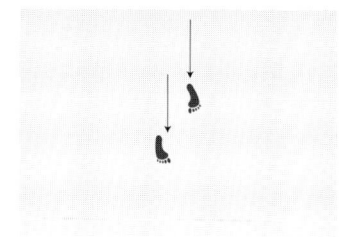

【㊹を東から見る】
㊹から直ちに肩の高さに引く

From ㊹ pull bach Uraken to the shoulder height.
㊹ seen from east.

足の動作●右足を前（南）へ1歩踏み出す。
立ち方●右基立ち。
手の動作●左手は開いて体の前へ出し、右内受けを左掌に当てる

着眼点●南

1: Take right foot one step forward (toward south).
2: Right-Motodachi
3: Put left hand open in front of the body, hit it against Right-Uchiuke.
4: South

足の動作●前へ寄り足にて進む。
立ち方●右基立ち。
手の動作●右裏拳にて上段を打つ。

着眼点●南

1: Step forward with drag(Yoriashi).
2: Right-Motodachi
3: Hit toward Jyodan with Right-Uraken, and pull back toward shoulder height immediately.
4: South

挙動の分解32、33   Seienchin Kumite in detail

中段突きしてくるのを、前足を後方へ引くと同時に、右中段内受け

㉑

Hitting opponent's Chudan-tsuki sideways with Chudan-uchiuke, while withdrawing front foot.

ただちに右拳で顔面へ裏打ちする。

㉒

Counter with Right-Urauchi to his face.

34挙動

⑥

⑦

⑧

【⑰を北東から見る】
⑰ seen from northeast.

足の動作●前足（右）を左足前に移動する。
立ち方●左三戦立ちになる途中。
手の動作●⑮のまま。

足の動作●体を北東へ回す。
立ち方●左三戦立ち。
手の動作●左中段外受け、右手は体の下方（正中線）へ伸ばして構える。

着眼点●北東

1:Bring front (right) foot in front of left foot.
2:On the way to Left-Sanchindachi
3:Same as in ㊹.
4:South

1:Turn body toward northeast.
2:Left-Sanchindachi
3:While executing Left-Chudan-Sotouke with left fist, stretch right hand toward lower part of body and hold there. (Seichu-sen)
4:Northeast

35挙動

【㊾を北東から見る】

㊾ seen from northeast.

足の動作●㊼のまま。
立ち方●左三戦立ち。
手の動作●左手を開いて掌を前に向けて掛け手をする。

留意点●左中段外受けから左掛け手に移るとき左手は上下動させないこと。

着眼点●北東

1:Same as in ㊼.
2:Left-Sanchindachi
3:Open left hand and execute Kakate, with palm facing forward.
4:Northeast

Point:Don't move left hand up and down while executing from Left-Chudan-Sotouke to Left-Kakete.

36挙動

【(51)を北西から見る】

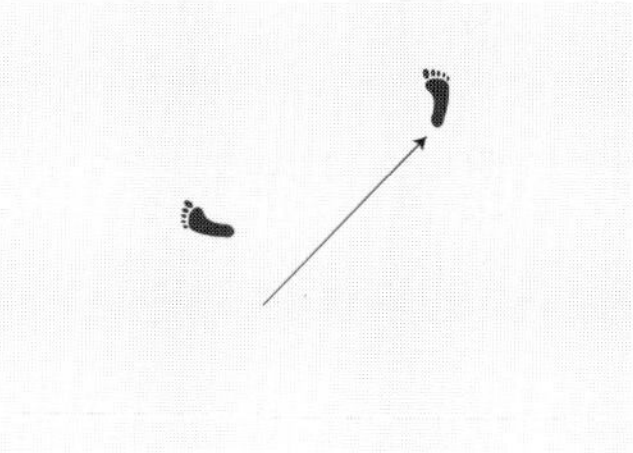

Agetsuki in (51), as seen from westnorth.

足の動作●右足を北東へ1歩運ぶ。
立ち方●四股立ち。
手の動作●右拳で上段揚突き、左手は開いて手首を立て掌を外に向けて水月前に構える。

備考●揚突きは相手の顎（あご）のあたりに当てる。揚突きした拳は直ちに肩の高さに引く。

着眼点●北東

1:Take right foot one step toward northeast.
2:Shikodachi
3:Execute Agetsuki with right fist, while bending wrist upward, hold left hand in front of abdomen, with palm facing forward.
4:Northeast

Note:Agetsuki should hit around opponent's jaw.After Agetsuki, fist should be pulled back to shoulder height immediately.

挙動の分解34～39・42～47　Seienchin Kumite in detail

中段突きを、左中段外受け。

Block opponent's Right-Chudan-tsuki with Left-Chudan-Uke from inside, while withdrawing front foot.

相手の手首を捕り、

After Chudan-Uke, turn around left wrist to grab his right wrist.

四股立ちになり右手を下に引きつけ、同時に右拳で顎（あご）に揚げ突きする。

While pulling his right hand downward at Shikodachi, execute Agetsuki to his jaw with right fist.

37挙動

セイエンチン

38挙動

【53を南東から見る】
裏打ちした拳は直ちに
肩の高さに引く

53 seen from southeast.
Pull bach the fist of Urauchi
to the shoulder height.

足の動作●51のまま。
立ち方●四股立ち。
手の動作●右上段裏打ち。

留意点●揚突きから上段裏打ち・下段払いの時上体が前後に振れないこと。

着眼点●北東

1: Same as in 51.
2: Shikodachi
3: Hit Right-Jyodan-Urauchi.
4: Northeast

Point: While executing from Agetsuki to Jyodan-Urauchi and Gedanbarai, don't move up and down of upper body.

足の動作●51のまま。
立ち方●四股立ち。
手の動作●右手で下段払いをする。水月前の左手は脇へ引く。

着眼点●北東

1: Same as in 51.
2: Shikiodachi
3: Execute Right-Gedanbarai fist. Pull back left hand in front of abdomen to the left side of the body.
4: Northeast

---

26 右拳で顔面に裏打ちする。 
After Agetsuki, execute Urauchi to his face with right fist.

27 相手がさらに中段突きしてくるのを、右拳で下段払い。 
Block his further Chudantsuki with right Gedanuke by hitting his left hand sideways.

28 続いてくる中段蹴りを、前足を右斜め後方へ引き左手で下段払い。 
Block his further Left-Chudan-geri with left Gedanuke, while withdrawing front foot.

29 右中段突きを脇腹へ極める。 
Finish with Right-Chudantsuki to his left side of body.

▶セイエンチン篇　129

39挙動　　40挙動

足の動作●右足を南西へ引く。
立ち方●四股立ち。
手の動作●左下段払いを行い、右拳は脇へ引く。

着眼点●北東

1: Pull back right foot toward southwest.
2: Shikodachi
3: Execute Left-Gedan-Uke fist. Pull back right fist to right side of body.
4: Northeast

足の動作●右足を左足の前へ引き、更に右足を少し引いて踵をあげる。
立ち方●右猫足立ち。
手の動作●両手の肘を前後に引くようにして、右肘は腕を肩の高さにあげ、左肘は後方へ当てる。

着眼点●南

1: Pull back right foot in front of left foot, then, pull back right foot a little more and lift up its heel.
2: Right-Nekoashidachi
3: Pulling both elbows apart from each other, lift right elbow up to shoulder height and push left elbow backward.
4: South

【57を東から見る】

57 seen from east.

留意点●前の肘はハズシ技であるからコースに留意。（当ての動作にならないこと）

備考●普通の猫足立ちよりやや腰を落とし、尻を後ろへ出すようにする。

Point: Front elbow is an evading technique and its moving route should be done carefully (Don't take hitting action)

Note: Hips are lower than usual Nekoashidachi and push buttocks slightly backward.

挙動の分解40、41・48、49
Seienchin Kumite in detail

後方より相手に組みつかれる。

Being held from behind.

41挙動

(59)

足の動作●右足を後ろ（北）へ引き、左足はすこし引いて踵をあげる。
立ち方●左猫足立ち。
手の動作●左腕は肘を前にして肩の高さにあげ、右肘は後方へ当てる。

着眼点●南

1:Pull right foot backward (toward north) and lift left heel up, after pulling back left foot slightly.
2:Left-Nekoashidachi
3:While lifting left arm until elbow comes to shoulder height and facing forward, execute right elbow attack backward with right arm.
4:South

(60)

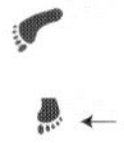

足の動作●前足（左）を右足前に移動する。
立ち方●右三戦立ちになる途中。
手の動作●(59)のまま。

着眼点●南

1:Bring front (left) foot toward inside and in front of right foot.
2:On the way to Right-Sanchindachi
3:Same as in (59).
4:South

猫足立ちのように腰を落とし、尻を後ろへ出し、右腕は肩の高さにあげて相手の腕をはずし、左肘当て。

㉛

Lowering hips and pushing buttocks backward like Nekoashidachi , lift right arm until shoulder height to unlock opponent's arm and hit backward with left elbow.

42挙動

(61)

足の動作●体を北西に向ける。
立ち方●右三戦立ち。
手の動作●右手は中段外受けを行い、左手は伸ばして体の下方（正中線）に構える。

着眼点●北西

1:Turn body toward northwest.
2:Right-Sanchindachi
3:While executing Right-Chudan-Sotouke, stretch left hand toward lower part of the body and hold there.
4:Northwest

後方へ向き中段突き。

㉜

Turn around immediately and finish with Right-Chudan-tsuki.

43挙動　　　44挙動　　　45挙動

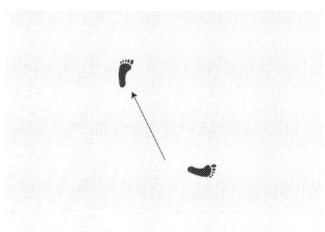

⑥　　　　　　⑥　　　　　　⑥

足の動作●⑥のまま。
立ち方●右三戦立ち。
手の動作●中段受けした右手を開き、掌を前に向けて掛け手をする。

着眼点●北西

足の動作●左足を北西へ1歩進め、腰を落とす。
立ち方●四股立ち。
手の動作●左拳で揚突きを行い、右手は開いて手首を立て、掌を前に向けて水月前に構える。

着眼点●北西

足の動作●⑥のまま。
立ち方●四股立ち。
手の動作●左上段裏打ちを行う。

着眼点●北西

1:Same as in ⑥.
2:Right-Sanchindachi
3:Opening right hand after finishing Chudan-Uke, execute Kakete-Uke, with palm facing forward.
4:Northwest

1:Take left foot a step toward northwest and lower hips.
2:Shikodachi
3:Execute Agetsuki with left fist, while bending wrist upward, hold right hand in front of abdomen, with palm facing forward.
4:Northwest

1:Same as in ⑥.
2:Shikodachi
3:Execute Left-Jyodanurauchi.
4:Northwest

セイエンチン

46挙動

足の動作●❻❸のまま。
立ち方●四股立ち。
手の動作●左下段払いを行い、右拳は脇へ引く。

着眼点●北西

1:Same as in ❻❸.
2:Shikodachi
3:Execute Left-Gedanbarai with left fist. Pull back right fist to right side of the body.
4:Northwest

47挙動

足の動作●右足を軸にして左足を後方(南東)へ引く。
立ち方●四股立ち。
手の動作●右下段払い。左手は脇へ引く。

着眼点●北西

1:Pivoting on the right foot pull left foot backward (toward southeast).
2:Shikodachi
3:Execute Right-Gedanbarai. Pull back left fist to left side of the body.
4:Northwest

48挙動

足の動作●左足を右足前に引いて踵をあげて腰を落とす。
立ち方●左猫足立ち。
手の動作●左手は肘を前にして肩の高さにあげ、右手は後方へ肘当てをする。

着眼点●南

1:Pull back left foot in front of right foot, then, lift left heel and lower hips.
2:Left-Nekoashidachi
3:While lifing left arm until elbow is shoulder height and facing forward, execute elbow attack backward with right arm.
4:South

49挙動

足の動作●左足を後方(北)へ引き、右足は少し引いて踵をあげる。
立ち方●右猫足立ち。
手の動作●右腕は肘を前にして肩の高さにあげ、左肘で後方へ当てる。

着眼点●南

1:Pull left foot backward (toward north) and draw back right foot a little and lift right heel.
2:Right-Nekoashidachi
3:While lifing right arm until elbow comes to shoulder height and facing forward, execute elbow attack backward with left arm
4:South

▶セイエンチン篇 133

50挙動

⑥⑨

⑦⑩ 【⑥⑨を東から見る】
⑥⑨ seen from east.

足の動作●⑥⑧のまま。
立ち方●右猫足立ち。
手の動作●左手を開いて手首を立てて右手の上より掌底にて中段を押さえる。

留意点●左掌底押さえた所から動かないこと。

着眼点●南

1: Same as in ⑥⑧.
2: Right-Nekoashidachi
3: Open left hand and bend wrist upward on top of the right fist, then, press Chudan with Shotei.
4: South

Point: Don't move from where Left-Shotei is executed.

51挙動

⑦①

⑦② 【⑦①を東から見る】
⑦① seen from left side.

足の動作●猫足立ちのまま前足(踵から)から波足で前に進む。
立ち方●右猫足立ち。
手の動作●波足で進みながら上段に右拳で裏打ちをし、直ちに肩の高さへ引く。

着眼点●南

1: With the same Nekoashidachi stance, stop forward with drag, from front foot first.
2: Right-Nekoashidachi
3: While stepping with drag (Namiashi), execute Urauchi toward Jyodan with right fist, then, pull back it to shoulder height immediately.
4: South

挙動の分解50〜52　Seienchin Kumite in detail

㉝ 中段突きを、猫足立ちて左手掌底にて下に押さえ。 
To counter opponent's Right-Chudantsuki, withdraw front foot to become Nekoashidachi and, at the same time, pressing downward with Left-Shotei.

㉞ 右拳にて顔面へ裏打ち。 
Execute Urauchi to his face with right fist.

㉟ 空いた脇へさらに中段突きしてくるのを、内側より肘を入れて受ける。 
Block his further Left-Chudan-tsuki to the open side of body with right elbow from inside. (Hijikuriuke)

㊱ 腰を落として四股立ちとなり、脇を肘当てで極め。
Lower hips to become Shikodachi and finish with right elbow attack to his left side of body.

セイエンチン
52挙動

⑦③ 【⑦③を東から見る】
⑦③ seen from east.

⑦④

⑦⑤

足の動作●右足を後方（北）へ引く。
立ち方●猫足立ちになる途中。
手の動作●裏打ちの状態から右手を引いて両肘を合わせるようにし。

着眼点●南

足の動作●ひき続き右足を引き、左足の踵をあげる。
立ち方●左猫足立ち。
手の動作●両肘を体の前で合わせ、さらに両肘を左右に張る。両掌は合わせ山型となる。（肘繰り受け）

留意点●猫足立ちに極まってからの肘繰り受け、両肘は繰り受けのコースを通すこと。
備考●⑦①の右裏打ちから、右足を引いて左猫足立ち、肘繰り受けの動作は連動のこと。

着眼点●南

1: Pull right foot backward (toward north).
2: On the way to stand Nekoashi-dachi.
3: Pull both hands toward face and put both elbows together.
4: South

1: Next, Pulling back right foot, then, lift left up heel.
2: Left-Nekoashidachi
3: Face both elbows in front of the body and spread both elbows to both sides of body, and tips of hands touching, form a "mountain" with palms. (Hijikuri-Uke)
4: South
Point: At performance of Hijikuriuke after finishing Nekoashidachi, both elbows should follow the Uke route.
Note: Actions from Right-Urauchi of ⑦① to Left-Nekoashidachi by pulling back right foot and Hijikuriuke should be in a linked way.

▶セイエンチン篇 135

止め　　　　　直立

⑦⑥　　⑦⑦　　⑦⑧

足の動作●左足を右足に引きつける。
立ち方●結び立ち。

手の動作●両手を合わせたまま下腹前におろす。

着眼点●南

足の動作●⑦⑥のまま。
立ち方●結び立ち。
手の動作●両手をそれぞれ体の両側に伸ばす。

着眼点●南

1:Pull left foot to the right foot.
2:Musubidachi

3:With both hands together, place them in front of lower abdomen.
4:South

1:Same as in ⑦⑥
2:Musubidachi
3:Stretch hands on both sides of the body, with arms and fingers straight down.
4:South

バッサイ(大)篇

〔特徴〕

　バッサイ・(大)は首里手の系統の形であり、基本技が集約され、攻防技の動作が連続的に組み合わされている。
　軽快な動きのなかに、技の切り返し、強弱の使い方、敏速な極め技等の流れが求められる。

BASSAI(DAI) is a KATA of Syurite system summing up basic techniques with combination of attack and defense in serial movements.
In the agile movements, counterattack, hard and soft strength and swift decisive techniques must be mastered.

※従来の中段横受けを、中段外受けに、中段横打ち受けを、中段内受けに統一した。
※Traditional Chudan Yokouke is changed into Chudan Sotouke and Chudan Yokouchiuke is changed into Chudan Uchiuke respectively.

BASSAI(DAI)

直立　　用意　　1挙動

【❸を西から見る】
❸ seen from west.

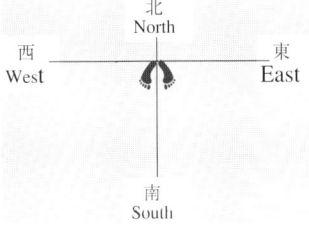

足の動作●踵をつけ爪先を開く。
立ち方●結び立ち。
手の動作●両手は開いて大腿部両側につけて伸ばす。

着眼点●南

1:Feet
2:Stance
3:Hands
4:Point to see

1:Put heels together, with toes apart.
2:Musubidachi
3:Open hands, stretch arms and fingers on both sides of the body.
4:South

足の動作●直立姿勢の位置で爪先をつける。
立ち方●閉足立ち。
手の動作●右拳は軽く握り、左手は開いて右手を包み下腹部に構える。

着眼点●南

1:Whithout changing upright position, put toes together.
2:Heisokudachi
3:Clench right fist lightly and wrapping right fist with left palm, hold them in front of abdomen.
4:South

足の動作●右足を南方へ1歩踏み出し左足を右足へ引きつける。
立ち方●右交差立ち。
手の動作●右手で中段外受けを行い、左手は開いて右拳の内側より掌にて押すようにして添える。(右中段拳支え受け)

着眼点●南

1:Take right foot one step toward south, then, pull left foot to the right foot.
2:Kosadachi
3:While executing Chudan-Sotouke with right fist, place left hand on right fist as if pressing with palm from inside. (Right-Chudan-Kensasaeuke)
4:South

挙動の分解1　Bassai(Dai) Kumite in detail

構え姿勢。

Kamae posture

中段突きを、斜め後方に前足を引いて右中段拳支え受け。

When opponent attacks with Right-Chudantsuki, pull front foot diagonally backward and execute Chudan-Kensasaeuke with right fist.

左手で相手の腕を押さえ右拳で上段へ裏打ちする。

While holding his right arm with left hand, execute Jyodan-Urauchi with right fist.

138

バッサイ（大）

2 挙動

⑤

【⑤を東から見る】
⑤ seen from east.

足の動作●左足を後方（北）へ1歩踏み出す。
立ち方●左前屈立ち。
手の動作●左中段外受け。右拳は脇へ引く。

着眼点●北

1: Take left foot one step toward north.
2: Left-Zenkutsudachi
3: Left-Chudan-Sotouke with left fist. Pull back right fist to right side of body.
4: North

留意点●
横への広い運足は要注意
広い

Point: Don't move sideway with wide stride.

3 挙動

⑦

【⑦を東から見る】
⑦ seen from east.

足の動作●左足を後方（南）へ一足分引きつける。
立ち方●左基立ち。
手の動作●右中段外受け左拳は左脇へ引く。

着眼点●北

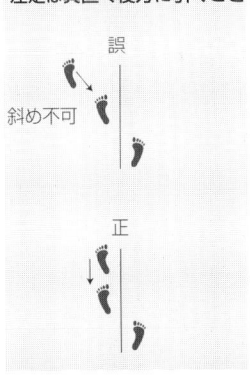

1: Pull left foot one step backward (toward south)
2: Left-Motodachi
3: Left-Chudan-Sotouke wih right fist. Pull back left fist to left side of the body.
4: North
Point: Left foot must pull back straight (not diagonally).

留意点●
左足は真直ぐ後方に引くこと
誤
斜め不可
正

挙動の分解 2〜3　Bassai(Dai) Kumite in detail

④
中段突きを、前屈立ちで、左中段外受け。

When opponent attacks with Right-Chudantsuki, shift body diagonally backward to right side and execute Left-Chudan-Sotouke.

⑤
左逆突きを、左足を引き、基立ちとなり、右中段外受け。

Block his further Left-Gyakutsuki with Right-Chudan-Sotouke by Motodachi with drawing back left foot.

⑥
中段突きで極める。

Counter and finish with Left-Chudantsuki.

▶バッサイ（大）篇　139

4 挙動

⑨ ⑩

【⑨を東から見る】

⑨ seen from east.

足の動作●右足を後方（南）へ踏み出す。
立ち方●右前屈立ち。
手の動作●左中段内受け、右拳は脇へ引く。

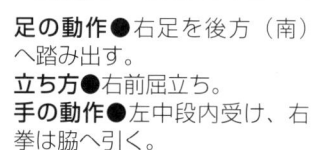

着眼点●南

1: Step right foot backward (toward south).
2: Right-Zenkutsudachi
3: Left-Chudan-Uchiuke. Pull right fist to right side of the body.
4: South

5 挙動

⑪ ⑫

【⑪を東から見る】

⑪ seen from east.

足の動作●右足を後方（北）へ一足分引く。
立ち方●右基立ち。
手の動作●右中段外受け、左拳は脇へ引く。

留意点●❺〜❼に同じ、運足に留意のこと。

着眼点●南

1: Pull right foot one step backward (toward north).
2: Right-Motodachi
3: Right-Chudan-Sotouke with right fist. Pull back left fist to left side of the body.
4: South

Point: Same as in ❺〜❼ Pay attention to foot movement.

挙動の分解 4、5　Bassai(Dai) Kumite in detail

中段突きを、前屈立ちとなり、中段内受け。

⑦

Block opponent's Right-Chudantsuki by hitting with Right-Chudan-Uchiuke, while pulling body diagonally backward to Zenkutsudachi.

中段逆突きを、左足を引き、基立ちとなり、左中段外受け。

⑧

Block his further Left-Chudan-Gyakutsuki with Motodachi by drawing back left foot and Left-Chudan-Sotouke.

中段突きで極める。

⑨

Counter with Right-Chudan-tsuki.

バッサイ（大）

6 挙動

⑬

⑭ 【⑬を西から見る】
⑬seen from west.

⑮ 足の動作●右足を後方へ引いて四股立ちのようになり、右足を左足に引き寄せて外八字立ちとなる。
立ち方●四股立ちより外八字立ち。
手の動作●右腕にて下より掬いあげるようにして上にあげる。右拳の高さは右耳の高さとする。

留意点●右手で下より掬いあげ、外八字立ちになると同時に西を見る。それまでは南を見る。

着眼点●南より西

⑯ 【⑮を西から見る】
右拳は耳の高さ
Right fist is at the ear level height.

足の動作●右足を後方（北）へ引いて四股立ちとなる。
立ち方●四股立ち。
手の動作●右腕で下方より掬いあげる。

備考●この動作は掬い止めへの移行動作であり、連続して行う。

着眼点●南

1:Pull right foot backward (toward north) to hold Shikodachi.
2:Shikodachi
3:Scoop upward with right arm.
4:South

Note:This movement is a serial switchover movement to scoop upward (Sukuidome).

1:Pull right foot backward to become like Shikodachi, then, pull right foot toward left foot to become Soto-Hachijidachi.
2:From Shikodachi to Soto-Hachijidachi
3:Raise right arm from underneath as if scooping upward. Right fist is at the ear level height.
4:From south to west

Point:Scooping upward with right arm from beneath and becoming Soto-Hachijidachi, with facing west. Until then, look toward south.

挙動の分解 6
Bassai(Dai)
Kumite in detail

⑩ 右中段蹴りを、斜め左前方へ入りながら右前腕で掬い。
Block opponent's Right-Chudangeri by scooping his leg with right forearm, while stepping in forward to left side.

⑪ 左手で左頸部へ左拳槌にて打ち。
Stretch left arm and hook left fist on his left side of neck.

⑫ 右前腕で足を上にあげ、頸部を下に押さえ。
Lift his right leg upward and push his neck downward.

⑬ 左右の足を引いて相手を投げる。
Pull back both feet and throw opponent to the ground.

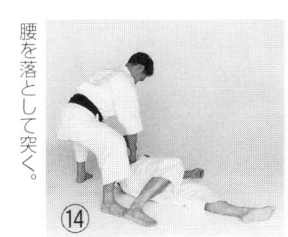

⑭ 腰を落として突く。
Lower hips and finish with Right-Tsuki, when he is thrown to the ground.

7 挙動

⑰

足の動作●右足の踵を浮かせて前へ出し、腰を落とす。
立ち方●右猫足立ち。
手の動作●右中段内受け、左拳はそのまま。

留意点●猫足立ちを崩さないこと。
着眼点●西

1: Lift right heel and step right foot forward, then, lower hips.
2: Right-Nekoashidachi
3: Right-Chudan-Uchiuke, left fist is held right there.
4: West
Point: Keep up Nekoashidachi.

8 挙動

⑱

足の動作●⑰のまま。
立ち方●右猫足立ち。
手の動作●左中段外受け、右拳は脇へ引く。

着眼点●西

1: Same as in ⑰.
2: Right-Nekoashidachi
3: Left-Chudan-Sotouke. Pull back right fist to right side of the body.
4: West

9 挙動

⑲

足の動作●右足を左へ移動し、両上足底を軸にして八字立ちとなる。
立ち方●外八字立ち。
手の動作●右拳は脇へ引き、左腕は拳の甲を上にして前腕を水平にして水月の前に構える。（右脇構え）

留意点●猫足立ちから外八字立ちにかわる場合の歩幅に注意。
⑱〜⑲動作への移り
着眼点●南

1: Pivoting both foot soles after right foot moved toward left to Hachijidachi
2: Soto-Hachijidachi
3: Pull back right fist to right side of the body. Put left forearm in front of abdomen horizontally, with back of left hand facing upward.
4: South
Point: Pay attention to the width of steps in the actions from Nekoashidachi to Soto-Hachijidachi(⑱ to ⑲).

挙動の分解 7、8　Bassai(Dai) Kumite in detail

⑮ 中段突きを、猫足立ち となり、中段内受け

Block opponent's Right-Chyudantsuki by hitting sideways with right Chudan-Uchiuke, while taking Nekoashidachi stance.

⑯ さらに中段逆突きで攻撃してくるのを、左中段外受け。

Block his further Left-Chudan-Gyakutsuki with Left-Chudan-Uke.

⑰ 右中段突き。

Taking Motodachi stance, counter with Right-Chudan-tsuki.

10挙動

⑳

【⑳を東から見る】
㉑ seen from east.

左横払いは肩の高さ
Left Yoko Barai is at height of shoulder.

足の動作●両足爪先を南西に向ける。両足がやや平行となる。
立ち方●
手の動作●左腕にて横に打ち払う（左中段横払い）。

備考●両足爪先を南西に向けると同時に上体を半身にする。

着眼点●南

1: Turn both toes toward southwest. Both feet become, more or less, parallel toward southwest.
3: Hit sideways with left arm (Left-Chudan-Yokobarai)
4: South

Note: While both toes pointing toward southwest, upper body becomes Hanmi.

バッサイ（大）
11挙動

㉒

足の動作●両足爪先を元に⑲にもどす。
立ち方●外八字立ち。
手の動作●右中段突き、左拳は脇へ引く。

着眼点●南

1: Return both toes to the initial position as in ⑲.
2: Soto-Hachijidachi
3: Right-Chudantsuki. Pull back left fist to left side of body.
4: South

挙動の分解 9〜14　Bassai(Dai) Kumite in detail

中段突きを、右拳槌および前腕で横に打ち払う。

⑱

Block opponent's Right-Chudantsuki by scooping his leg with right forearm, while stepping in forward to left side.

左中段突きを、右中段突きで突き受け。

⑲

Block his further Left-Chudantsuki and counter-attack with Right-Chudantsuki from beneath.

▶バッサイ（大）篇　143

12挙動

㉓
㉔【㉓を東から見る】

㉓ seen from east.

足の動作●両足爪先を南東に向ける。両足は南東に向かってやや平行となる。
立ち方●
手の動作●右中段外受けを行う。
留意点●腰の回転に乗せながら右中段受けにかわる。右拳を引くだけで受けに変わるのは不可。
備考●中段受けを行うと同時に上体は半身となる。
㉒㉓は連続動作。
着眼点●南

1: Turn both toes toward southeast. Each foot becomes, more or less, parallel toward southeast.
3: Right-Chudan-Sotouke.
4: South

Note: While executing Chudan-Uke, upper body becomes Hanmi. ㉒ and ㉓ must be a continuous movement.
Point: Change into Right-Chudan-Uke with body turn. Don't change into Right-Chudan-Uke with pulling back right fist only.

13挙動

㉕

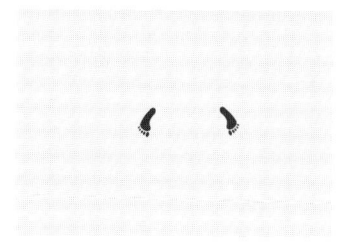

足の動作●両足爪先を元に㉒にもどす。
立ち方●外八字立ち。
手の動作●左中段突き、右拳は脇へ引く。

着眼点●南

1: Return both toes to initial position as in ㉒.
2: Soto-Hachijidachi
3: Left-Chudantsuki. Pull back right fist to right side of body.
4: South

中段突きを、右中段外受け。
㉒ Block his further Right-Chudan-tsuki with Right-Chudan-Sotouke.

左中段突き。
㉑ Counter with Left-Chudan-tsuki.

バッサイ（大）

14挙動

㉖

㉗

【㉖を東から見る】

㉖ seen from east.

足の動作●両足爪先を南西に向ける。
立ち方●
手の動作●左中段外受けを行う。

着眼点●南

1:Turn both toes toward southwest.
3:Left-Chudan-Sotouke.
4:South

㉘

足の動作●右足を前方へ半歩出す。
立ち方●右猫足立ち。
手の動作●右手を開いて、甲を下にして体の前から前腕を水平にする。

着眼点●南

1:Take right foot half step out toward south.
2:Right-Nekoashidachi
3:Open right hand, back of hand facing downward, and hold forearm in front of chest horizontally.
4:South

15挙動　　16挙動　　17挙動

㉙　　㉚　　㉛

足の動作●立ち方および位置そのまま。
立ち方●右猫足立ち。
手の動作●右手刀下段払い、左手は開いて甲を下に向け水月前に引く。
留意点●㉖～㉙最短距離を通って一挙動で動く。

着眼点●南

1: Same as in 28.
2: Right-Nekoashidachi[
3: Gedanbarai with Right-Shuto. Open left hand, with back of hand facing downward, and pull it in front of abdomen.
4: South
Point: Hands of ㉖ and ㉙ must move in one action by shortest route.

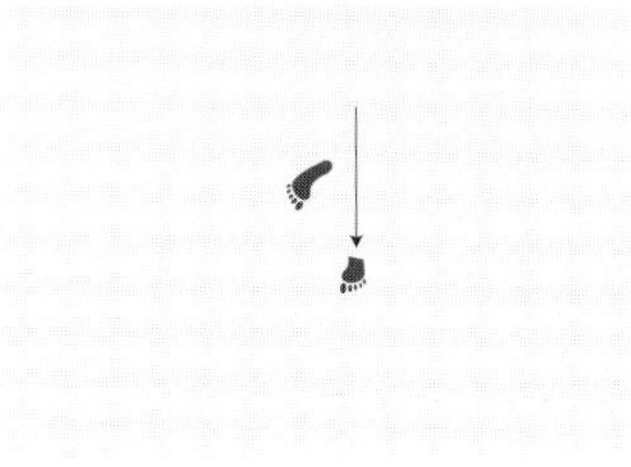

足の動作●左足を南へ出す。
立ち方●左猫足立ち。
手の動作●左手刀下段払い、右手は水月前に引く。

着眼点●南

1: Step out left foot toward south.
2: Left-Nekoashidachi
3: While executing Gedanbarai with Left-Shuto, pull up right hand in front of abdomen.
4: South

足の動作●右足を南へ出す。
立ち方●右猫足立ち。
手の動作●右手刀下段払い、左手は水月前に引く。

着眼点●南

1: Step out right foot toward south.
2: Right-Nekoashidachi
3: While executing Gedanbarai with Right-Shuto, pull up left hand in front of abdomen.
4: South

挙動の分解15～20　Bassai(Dai) Kumite in detail

㉒ 中段蹴りを、猫足立ち、左手刀下段払い となり、

Block opponent's Right-Chudan-geri with Left-Shuto-Gedan-barai, while withdrawing body diagonally to right side and taking Nekoashidachi stance.

㉓ 右中段突きを、左中段掛け手。

Block his further Right-Chudantsuki with Left-Chudan-kakete.

㉔ 左中段逆突きで攻撃してくるのを、左手を相手の突きの下より回して、掛け手で手首を捕り、右手で流し受けを行う。

Block his further Left-Chudan-tsuki by grasping his wrist with Kakete after moving left hand around his left hand, then, execute Nagashiuke with right hand.

バッサイ（大）

18挙動

③②

足の動作●右足を後ろ（北）へ引く。
立ち方●左猫足立ち。
手の動作●左中段掛け手、右手は甲を上にして水月前に引く。

着眼点●南

1: Pull right foot backward (toward north).
2: Left-Nekoashidachi
3: Left-Chudan-Kaketeuke. Pull up right hand, back of hand facing upward, in front of abdomen.
4: South

19挙動

③③

足の動作●③②のまま。
立ち方●左猫足立ち。
手の動作●左手をすこし下にさげてから中段掛け手を行いながら左胸（乳）まで引き、右手は開手で体の左側前に出して流し受けをする。

留意点●左右の手の動作は同時に行い、上体は半身となる。
左掛け手をそのまま中段に引き付けてはならない。

着眼点●南

1: Same as in ⑱.
2: Left-Nekoashidachi
3: Lower left hand slightly and, while executing Chudan-Kaketeuke, pull it to left chest, push right hand, with palm open, forward in front of left side of body and execute Nagashiuke.
4: South

Point: Movement of both hands must be done simultaneously. Upper body becomes Hanmi.
Don't pull Left-Kakete directly to Chudan.

③④

【㉝を東から見る】

㉝ seen from east.

上半身のみを半身になり左猫足立ちが崩れないこと。

Hold left Nekoashidachi firmly with Hanmi position by upper body only.

20挙動

㉟

【㉟を東から見る】
㉟ seen from east.

㊲

【㊲を東から見る】
㊲ seen from east.

足の動作●左足踵を下につけ、右足を左足の膝の上まであげる。
立ち方●
手の動作●前㉝のまま。

留意点●右足をあげたときに爪先を上に反らす。㉝から㊲への移行動作。

着眼点●南

1: While placing left heel firmly on the floor, lift right knee until the heel reaches knee height.
3: Some as in ㉝.
4: South

Point: When lifting right knee, bend toe upward.
Transition movement from ㉝ to ㊲.

足の動作●右の足刀を前（南）へ踏みおろす。
立ち方●外八字立ち。
手の動作●両手を握り、甲を上にして左腰の脇へ引きつける。

留意点●左脇をしっかりと締めて引き付けること。

着眼点●南

1: Put down right Sokuto forward (toward south).
2: Soto-Hachijidachi
3: Clenching both hands, back of hands facing upward, pull them to left hip.
4: South

Point: Pull back arms in squeezing to left side of body.

㉕
相手の腕を捕ると同時に、右足を上にあげ。
While grasping his left arm with right hand, lift right knee.

㉖
足刀を相手の膝の内側に当て、踏みおろす。 
Strike his inside of right knee with Sokuto of lifted right foot.

21挙動

㊴

㊵

【㊴を北から見る】
㊴ seen from north.

足の動作●後ろ（北）へ向き、左足をすこし引く。
立ち方●左猫足立ち。
手の動作●左中段手刀受け、右手は水月前に引く。

着眼点●北

1: Turn around body backward (toward north) and pull back left foot slightly.
2: Left-Nekoashidachi
3: Left-Chudan-Shutouke. Pull right hand in front of abdomen.
4: North

22挙動

㊶

㊷

【㊶を北から見る】
㊶ seen from north.

足の動作●右足を半歩前へ出す。
立ち方●右猫足立ち。
手の動作●右中段手刀受け。左手は水月前に引く。

1: Take right foot half step forward.
2: Right-Nekoashidachi
3: Right-Chudan-Shutouke. Pull left hand in front of abdomen.

挙動の分解21〜25　Bassai(Dai) Kumite in detail

中段突きを、猫足立ちとなり、手刀受け。

㉗

Block opponent's Right-Chudan-tsuki with Left-Shutouke, while withdrawing body diagonally to right side and taking Nekoashidachi stance.

▶バッサイ（大）篇　149

23挙動

㊸ ㊹

【㊸を北から見る】
㊸ seen from north.

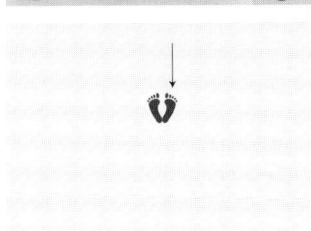

足の動作●右足を左足へ引きつける。
立ち方●閉足立ち。
手の動作●上段輪受け。右手を引き付け、両拳・両肘を締めながら上段輪受けに入る。上段輪受けのとき、肘を曲げること。

着眼点●北

1:Pull right foot to left foot.
2:Heisokudachi
3:Jyodan-Wauke
　Pulling right hand and clenching both fists and elbows to form Jyodan-Wauke. at Jyodan-Wauke the elbow has to bend.
4:North

24挙動

㊺ ㊻ ㊼

【㊺を北から見る】
㊺ seen from north.

【㊺を西から見る】
㊺ seen from west.

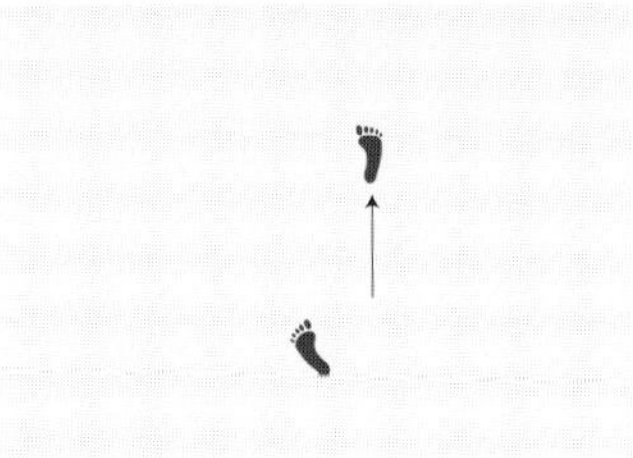

足の動作●右足を1歩踏み出す。
立ち方●右前屈立ち。
手の動作●左右の拳槌を中段へ打ち込む。

留意点●一歩踏み込んだときは、確実に前屈立ちになること。

着眼点●北

1:Take right foot a step forward.
2:Right-Zenkutsudachi
3:Hit toward Chudan with right and Left-Kentsui.
4:North

Point: When taking one step forward, Stand Zenkutsudachi firmly.

㉘ 左上段逆突きを、上段輪受け。

Block his further Left-Jyodan-Gyakutsuki with Jyodan-Wauke, bringing up both hands.

㉙ 右足を一歩踏み込んで、左右の拳槌で脇腹へ打ち込む。

Take right foot in a step toward opponent, then, hit at his both sides of body with both Kentsui.

㉚ 相手が体を後ろへ引いて拳槌打ちをかわしたら、四股立ちで踏み込み、右中段突きで極める。

If opponent pulls back body to dodge Kentsuiuchi, then, step in to become Shikodachi and finish with Right-Chudantsuki.

バッサイ（大）

25挙動

㊽ **㊾**

【㊽を西から見る】
㊽ seen from west.

足の動作●両足を前へすこしずらして進める。
立ち方●四股立ち。
手の動作●右拳で中段突き、左拳は脇へ引く。
備考●右拳の中段突きは肩の高さと同じ位置。
直ちに四股立ちに転ずる。この時右方向（北）に
少し寄り足。

着眼点●北

1:Move both feet forward a little.
2:Shikodachi
3:Chudantsuki with right fist. Pull back left fist to left side of the body.
4:North
Note:Chudantsuki with right fist must be on level of shoulder height.
Change into Shikodachi immediately with dragging a little toward nortth (Yoriashi).

26挙動

㊿ **(51)**

【㊿を西から見る】
㊿ seen from west.

足の動作●左足を右足へつける。
立ち方●閉足立ち。
手の動作●左下段払い、右拳は耳の高さに構える。
留意点●左右の前腕は体の中央で交差して、下段払いおよび構えを行う。
四股立ちから、閉足立ち・上段・下段の動作は一挙動。
ゆっくりは不可。

着眼点●南

1:Pull left foot to right foot together.
2:Heisokudachi
3:Left-Gedanbarai. Hold right fist on level of right ear height.
4:South
Point:After crossing both forearms in front of abdomen, execute Gedanbarai and Kamae. Movement from Shikodachi to Heisokudachi, Jyodan and Gedan must be done in a stroke.Slow movement must not be done.

挙動の分解26、27
Bassai(Dai) Kumite in detail

中段突きを、左手下段払い。

(31)

Block opponent's Right-Chudan tsuki with Left-Gedanbarai.

▶バッサイ（大）篇　151

27挙動

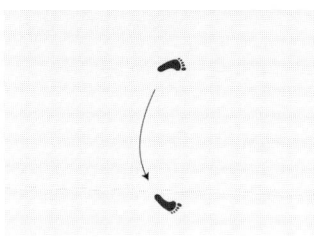

⑤②

【⑤②を東から見る】

⑤③ seen from east.

足の動作●右足を前（南）へ
1歩踏み出して腰を落とす。
立ち方●四股立ち。
手の動作●右下段払い、左手
は甲を上にして水月の高さに
水平に構える。

着眼点●北

1: Take right foot one step forward (toward south), then, lower hips.
2: Shikodachi
3: Right-Gedanbarai. Hold left forearm in front of abdomen horizontally, with back of left hand facing upward.
4: North

28挙動

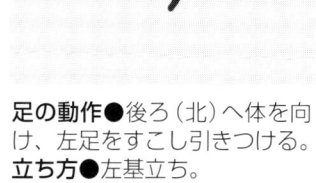

⑤④

【⑤④を東から見る】

⑤⑤ seen from east.

足の動作●後ろ（北）へ体を向
け、左足をすこし引きつける。
立ち方●左基立ち。
手の動作●左中段横払い、右
拳は脇へ引く。

着眼点●南

1: Turn around body backward (toward north) and pull back left foot slightly.
2: Left-Motodachi
3: Hit Left-Chudan-Yokobarai with left fist. Pull back right fist to right side of the body.
4: South

㉜ 左中段蹴りを、四股立ちとなり、右下段払い。

Block his further Left-Chudan-geri with Right-Gedanbarai, while withdrawing front foot diagonally to left side and taking Shikodachi stance.

㉝ 中段突き。

Counter with Left-Chudan-tsuki.

バッサイ（大）

29挙動

⑤⑥

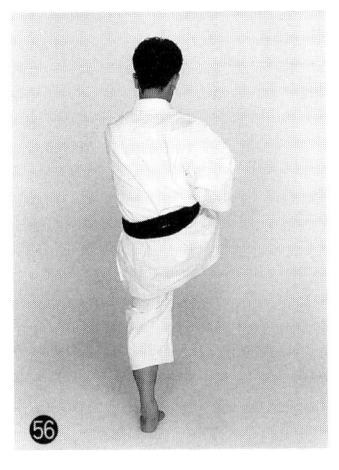

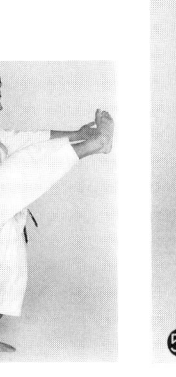

【⑤⑥を東から見る】
⑤⑥ seen from east.

足の動作●右足で左掌に当てるように回し蹴りする。
手の動作●右足の回し蹴りが当たるとき左拳を開く。

備考●回し蹴りの時、左拳は下げないこと。

着眼点●北

1:Mawashigeri with right foot, aiming to hit left palm.
3:Open left fist, when right foot Mawashigeri hits it.
4:North

Note: When Mawashigeri is executed, left fist must not lower down.

30挙動

⑤⑧

【⑤⑧を北から見る】
⑤⑧ seen from north.

足の動作●回し蹴りをした右足を前におろす。
立ち方●右前屈立ち。
手の動作●左前腕内側に対して、右肘当てを行う。

備考●右肘当ては甲を上にすること。

着眼点●北

1:After Mawashigeri, put down right foot forward.
2:Right-Zenkutsudachi
3:Right elbow attack against inside of left forearm.
4:North

Note: When right elbow attack is executed, back of righthand should be facing upward.

挙動の分解28〜30　Bassai(Dai) Kumite in detail

中段突きを、横払い。 
㉞
Block opponent's Right-Chudantsuki by Yokobarai.

相手の腕を捕りながら右中段蹴り。 
㉟
Execute Right-Chudangeri, while grabbing his right arm with left hand.

前屈立ちとなり、右肘で当てる。 
㊱
Take Zenkutsudachi stance, pulling his right arm under left armpit, then, hit right elbow toward his Chudan.

31挙動

⑥⓪

【⑥⓪を北から見る】
⑥⓪ seen from north.

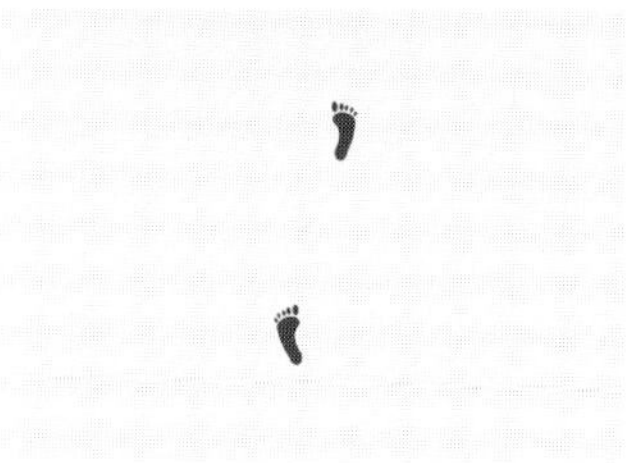

⑥①

足の動作●⑤⑧のまま。
立ち方●右前屈立ち。
手の動作●肘当てをした右手で下段払い、左拳は右肘関節の内側に構える。

留意点●3回の下段払いは1・2・3回とも等間隔で行う。

着眼点●北

1: Same as in ⑤⑧.
2: Right-Zenkutsudachi
3: After elbow attack, execute Gedanbarai with right fist. Hold left fist against inside of the right elbow.
4: North

Note: Three times execution of Gedanbarai must be done in a same interval..

**挙動の分解31〜39
Bassai(Dai) Kumite
in detail**

32挙動

⑥②

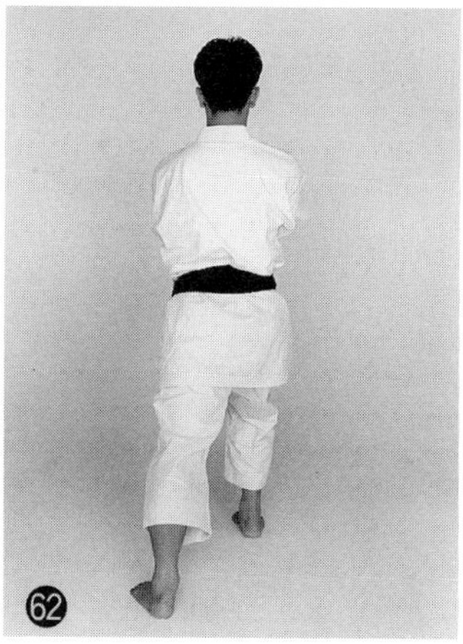

【⑥②を北から見る】
⑥② seen from north.

⑥③

足の動作●⑤⑧のまま。
立ち方●右前屈立ち。
手の動作●左下段払い、右拳は左肘の内側へ構える。

着眼点●北

1: Same as in ⑤⑧.
2: Right-Zenkutsudachi
3: Left-Gedanbarai. Hold right fist against inside of left elbow.
4: North

㊲ 中段突きを、左下段払い。 
Block opponent's Right-Chudan tsuki with Left-Gedanbarai.

㊳ 中段突きを、下段に払い。 
Block his further Left-Chudan-tsuki with Right-Gedanbarai.

バッサイ（大）

33挙動

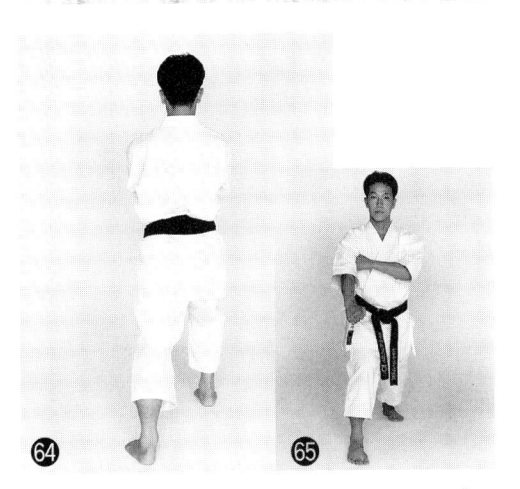

⑥④ ⑥⑤

足の動作●⑤⑧のまま。
立ち方●右前屈立ち。
手の動作●右下段払い、左拳は右肘の内側へ引いて構える。

留意点●⑥⓪⑥②⑥④の下段払いは連続して等間隔に行う。

着眼点●北

1: Same as in ⑤⑧.
2: Right-Zenkutsudachi
3: Right-Gedanbarai. Hold left fist against inside of right elbow.
4: North

Point: Execute Gedanbarai of ⑥⓪ ⑥② and ⑥④ consecutively in a same interval.

【⑥④を北から見る】
⑥④ seen from north.

34挙動

⑥⑥ ⑥⑦ ⑥⑧

足の動作●⑤⑧のまま。
立ち方●右前屈立ち。
手の動作●左右の両拳を左腰の脇へ引いて構える。（左脇構え）

留意点●双手突きのとき下足底（踵）があがらぬこと。

着眼点●北

1: Same as in ⑤⑧.
2: Right-Zenutsudachi
3: Pull back both fists to left side of the body and hold there. (Hidariwaki-Kamae)
4: North

Point: When Morotetsuki is executed, don't lift up bottom of foot(heel).

【⑥⑥を北から見る】
⑥⑥ seen from north.

【⑥⑥を西から見る】
⑥⑥ seen from west.

連続の右突きを、下段払い。

㊵
Block his further Right-Chudan-tsuki with Left-Gedanbarai.

上段突きを、右拳上段突き左拳裏突き。

㊵
Then, while bloking his further Left-Jyodantsuki with Right-Jyodantsuki and with Left-Uraken.

▶バッサイ（大）篇 155

35挙動

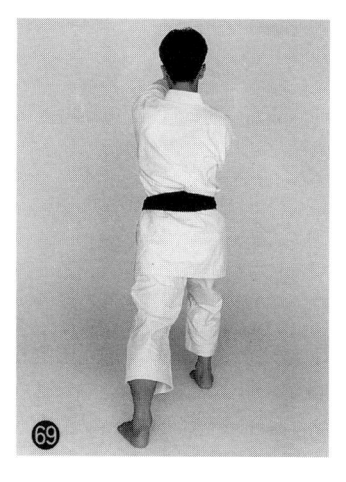

⑥⑨
⑦⑩

【⑥⑨を西から見る】
⑥⑨ seen from west.

足の動作●⑤⑧のまま。
立ち方●右前屈立ち。
手の動作●左拳上段突き、右拳は裏突きで同時に突く（双手突き）。

留意点●拳を引くとき下足底があがらぬこと。
双手突きの時、前の膝が決めの瞬間動かぬこと。
左拳と右拳の位置が上下対応すること

着眼点●北

1:Same as in ⑤⑧.
2:Right-Zenkutsudachi
3:While executing Jyodantsuki with left fist, execute Uratsuki with right fist simultaneously(Morotetsuki).
4:North
Point:When fist is pulled back don't lift up bottom of foot (heel).
When Morotetsuki is executed don't move front knee at the moment of Kime.
The position of right and left fist must correspond to up and down mutually.

36挙動

⑦①
⑦②

【⑦①を北から見る】
⑦① seen from north.

足の動作●右足を左足に引きつける。
立ち方●閉足立ち。
手の動作●左右の拳を右脇へ引いて構える。（右脇構え）

留意点●⑥⑨から右足を引き、閉足立ちになるとき左下足底があがらぬこと。

着眼点●北

1:Pull right foot to left foot.
2:Heisokudachi
3:Pull back both fists to right side of the body. (Right-Waki-Kamae)
4:North

Point:C:When right foot is pulled back from ⑥⑨ and become Heisokudachi don't lift up left bottom of foot.

バッサイ（大）

37挙動

⑦③

【⑦③を北から見る】
⑦④ ⑦③ seen from north.

足の動作●左足を北へ1歩踏み出す。
立ち方●左前屈立ち。
手の動作●右上段突き、左拳は裏突きを同時に行う（双手突き）。

着眼点●北

1: Take left foot one step forward to north.
2: Left-Zenkutsudachi
3: While executing Right-Jyodantsuki, with execute Left-Uratsuki at the same time(Morotetsuki).
4: North

38挙動

⑦⑤

【⑦⑤を北から見る】
⑦⑥ ⑦③ seen from north.

足の動作●左足を右足に引きつける。
立ち方●閉足立ち。
手の動作●左右の拳を左脇へ引いて構える（左脇構え）。

着眼点●北

1: Pull left foot to right foot.
2: Heisokudachi
3: Pull back both fists to left side of body. (Hidariwaki Kamae)
4: North

▶バッサイ（大）篇　157

39挙動

⑦

⑦⑧

【⑦を北から見る】
⑦ seen from north.

⑦⑨

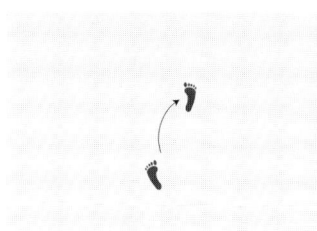

足の動作●右足を北へ１歩踏み出す。
立ち方●右前屈立ち。
手の動作●左上段突き、右拳は裏突きを同時に行う（双手突き）。

留意点●⑥⑥〜⑦⑦で下足底をあげないこと。

着眼点●北

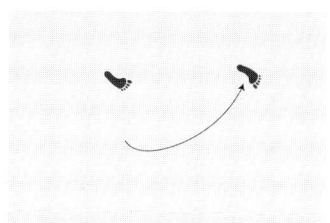

足の動作●右足を軸にして後方（南）へ体を回す。左膝は曲げ、右足は伸ばして立つ。両爪先は南東へ向く。
立ち方●前屈立ちのような立ち方
手の動作●右前腕にて下より掬うようにして体の左側面で止め（次へ連続動作）。

備考●腰の回転に乗せながら右拳を大きく振込んで中段振り捨てをする。

着眼点●南

1: Take right foot one step forward to north.
2: Right Zenkutsudachi
3: While executing Jyodantsuki with left fist, execute Uratsuki with right fist simultaneously. (Morotetsuki)
4: North

Point: Don't lift up bottom of foot from ⑥⑥ to ⑦⑦.

1: Pivoting on right foot, turn around body backward (toward south). Bend left knee and stretch right leg. Both toes point toward southeast.
2: Similar to Zenkutsudachi
3: Move right forearm as if scooping from beneath, then, hold on left side of body. (Continuous movement to next)
4: South

Note: While turning hips, execute right fist Furikomi-Chudan-Furisute.

40挙動

バッサイ（大）

⑧⑩
【⑧⑩を東から見る】
⑧⑩ seen from east.

⑧①

⑧②

足の動作●立ち方および位置はそのまま。
手の動作●左側で止めた右腕をただちに体の右側まで返す（振捨て）。

備考●⑦⑨の手の動作は連続する。このとき右手の甲を下にして前腕は水平とする。
⑦⑨⑧⑩の前腕を返すとき裏拳で下を打つような要領で止める。

1 : Same as in ⑦⑨.
3 : Return right forearm to right side of body quickly. (Furisute)

Note : Hands in ⑦⑨ must be a continuous movement. Back of right hand should be facing downward, while forearm is kept horizontal. When forearm of ⑦⑨⑧⑩ is turned back, stop it like hitting downward with Uraken.

足の動作●両爪先を南西に向け、右膝を曲げ、左膝を伸ばす。
立ち方●前屈立ちのような立ち方
手の動作●左腕を伸ばし体の右側まで振るようにして払う。

着眼点●南

1 : Both toes point toward southwest. Bend right knee and stretch left leg.
2 : Similar to Zenkutsudachi
3 : Stretch left forearm and bring it to right side of body in a swinging motion.
4 : South

挙動の分解40、41
Bassai(Dai) Kumite in detail

中段蹴りを、右前腕で内側に引っ掛け。

④①

When opponent attacks with Right-Chudangeri, pull front foot backward, then, hook his right foot on right forearm.

前腕をかえして。

④②

Turn around right forearm.

▶バッサイ（大）篇 159

41挙動

【❽❸を東から見る】

❽❸ seen from east.

足の動作●立ち方および位置はそのまま。
手の動作●払った左前腕を体の左側まで甲を下にして返す。このとき前腕を水平にする。

着眼点●南

1:Some as in ❽❷.
3:Turn and bring back swinging left forearm, back of hand facing downward to left side of body. Forearm is kept horizontal.
4:South

足の動作●左足を半歩斜め後ろ（北東）へ引く。
手の動作●前のまま。

着眼点●南

1:Pull left foot half step diagonally backward (toward northeast).
3:Same as in ❽❸.
4:South

体の外側に相手の足を振り捨てる。

Drop his right foot to right side of body.

背面に中段突き。

Counter immediately with Chudantsuki to his exposed back.

160

バッサイ（大）

42挙動

⑧⑥

⑧⑦

⑧⑧

足の動作●腰を落として右足踵をあげて左足方向へ引く。
立ち方●右猫足立ち。
手の動作●右中段掛け手。左手は甲を上にして水月前に構える。

着眼点●南西

1: Lower down hips, lift right foot heel and pull toward left foot.
2: Right-Nekoashidachi
3: Chudan-Kakieteuke with right hand. Hold left hand in front of abdomen, back of hand facing upward.
4: Southwest

足の動作●⑧⑥のまま。
立ち方●右猫足立ち。
手の動作●⑧⑥のまま。

備考●目付けのみ一挙動

着眼点●着眼点だけ南東

1: Same as in ⑧⑥.
2: Righit-Nekoashidachi
3: Same as in ⑧⑥.
4: Southeast

Note: Only Metsuke with one action

足の動作●右足を左足の斜め後方（北西）へ引く。
手の動作●両手を右足を引いた方向（北西）へ⑧⑦の高さのまま引く。

備考●右足爪先（上足底）は猫足立ちに変化するために右斜め前に向けておくこと。

着眼点●南東

1: Pull back right foot to back of left foot diagonally (toward northwest).
3: Pull back both hand with ⑧⑦ height toward northwest, together with right foot.
4: Southeast

Note: Face right foot toe toward diagonal front as it transfers to Nekoashidachi position.

挙動の分解42、43
Bassai(Dai) Kumite in detail

㊺ 中段突きを、猫足立ちとなり、掛け手。

Block opponent's Right-Chudan-tsuki with Right-Kaketeuke, while withdrawing front foot diaginally to left side and taking Nekoashidachi stance.

㊻ 相手の手首を捕り。

Grab his right wrist with right hand.

▶バッサイ（大）篇 161

43挙動　　　　　　　　　　　　　　止め

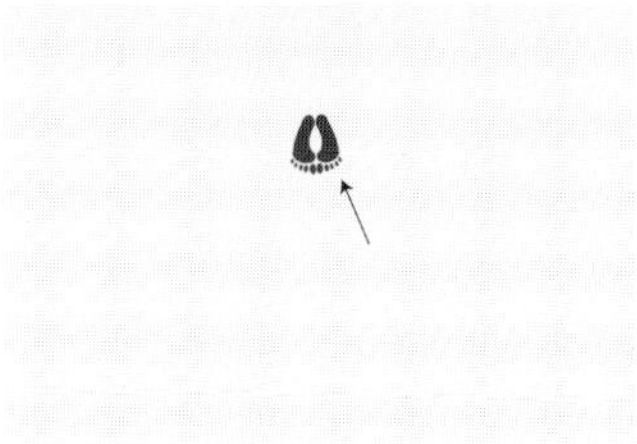

⑧⑨　　　　　　　　　　⑨⓪　　　　　　　　　　⑨①

足の動作●引いた右足の踵をつけ、左足踵をあげ、右足の方向へすこし引く。
立ち方●左猫足立ち。
手の動作●左中段掛け手。右手は甲を上にして水月前に構える。

着眼点●南東

1: Put down right heel, lift left heel and pull left foot to right foot slightly.
2: Left-Nekoashidachi
3: Chudan-Kaketeuke with left hand. Hold right hand facing upward in front of abdomen.
4: Southeast.

足の動作●左足を右足に引きつける。
立ち方●閉足立ち。
手の動作●右手は握り、左手は開いて右拳を包み、下腹部に構える。

着眼点●南東

1: Pull left foot to right foot together.
2: Heisokudachi
3: Clench right hand while wrapping right fist with left palm and hold them in front of abdomen.
4: Southeast

着眼点●南東より残心後、南

4: After Zanshin(a state of alertness in mind) move swiftly from southeast to south.

前足で中段蹴りする。

㊼

Chudangeri with front foot.

左中段突き。

㊽

Put down kicking right foot forward, then, execute Left-Chudantsuki to his left side of body.

162

直立

足の動作●両爪先を開く。
立ち方●結び立ち。
手の動作●両手をそれぞれ体の外側に伸ばす。

着眼点●南

1:Open both toes.
2:Musubidachi
3:Stretch both hands each outside of body respectively.
4:South

セイシャン篇

特徴
前半は全身の力を均等に使って技が止ることなくリズミカルに動作する。
後半は前半の応用動作で立ち方に特徴がある。

Specialty
①In first half of SEISHAN edition, movements should be done rythmically without stopping of waza in applying strength of whole body equally. Last half of this edition explains practical movements in application of first half edition with particular stance(tachikata).

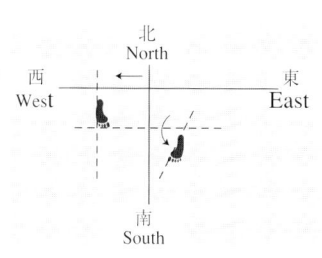

セイシャンの立ち方
①左右の足幅はナイハンチ立ち程度。
②前足先を内輪にし、後ろ足はごくわずかに内輪にする。体をすこし沈め、膝は柔らかにする。
③両足の前後の距離は、前足踵の後側と後足指先とが、ほとんど一直線上よりすこし前にあるように立つ。

Stance of SEISHAN
①Width between feet should be almost same as that of Naihanchidachi(standing naturally).
②Front foot points inward and also turns hind foot slightly inward. Lower body slightly and loosen knee joints.
③Tip of hind foot's big toe should be slightly in front of the line of back of front foot's heel.

セイシャンの進み方
①（左足前の場合）左足踵をすこし内転し、右足を内輪にしながら、内側から外側に幾分弧を描くように前に進め、前記の立ち方になる。
②体の重心をはずさず、上体を正面向きのまま、右足全体を柔らかに運ぶ。

Feet of SEISHAN
①(left foot in front)Turn left foot's heel slightly inward and, while turning right foot inward, advance it such like drawing a circle from inside to outside.
②Putting body gravity in between both feet with upper body facing front, advance right leg softly.

縦セイシャンの立ち方
①左右の足幅を少なくし、後足踵の内側縁と、前足拇指先縁が同一線上にあるように内輪にする。
②前後の足幅は、（横）セイシャン立ちをそのまま縦にした足幅程度となる。

Stance of TATE-SEISHAN
①Reduce width between both feet, inside of hind heel and tip of front foot's big toe (facing inward) should be on the same line.
②Width between foot should be same as that of Seishandachi.

SEISHAN

直立

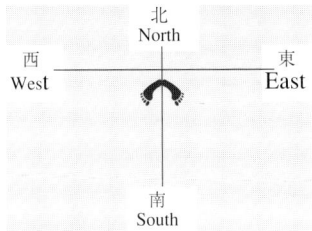

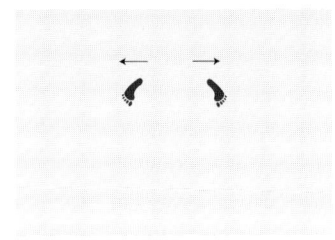

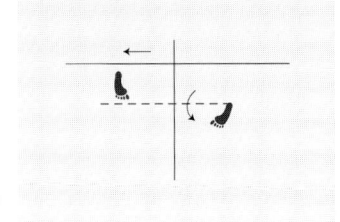

足の動作●結び立ち。
立ち方●結び立ち。
手の動作●両手は開いて、大腿部前に軽く垂れる。

着眼点●南

Remarks
1:Feet
2:Stance
3:Hands
4:Point to see

1:Musubidachi
2:Musubidachi
3:Open both hands and place them in front of thighs.
4:South

用意

足の動作●結び立ちから足を左、右と開き、八字立ちとなる（両踵の間隔は1足長半）。
立ち方●八字立ち。
手の動作●両手は大腿部前で軽く握る。

着眼点●南

1:Open left foot and then right foot(width of heels is a foot and half apart)to stand Hachijidachi
2:Hachijidachi
3:Grip both hands lightly in front of thighs.
4:South

足の動作●右踵をやや外転し、左足を内輪にし、内側より弧を描きながら南に進める。
立ち方●左セイシャン立ち（左足踵の後側の横一線より、右足先がすこし前に出る程度に立つ）。
手の動作●両拳を胸前で交差（右腕上）しながら、足が極まると同時に満身の力を入れて動作に入る。

着眼点●南

1:Turn right foot's heel outward a little while turning left foot inward, advance it to south as if drawing a circle from inside.
2:Left-Seishandachi (tip of right foot's big toe should be slightly in front of the line of back of left heel).
3:While crossing both arms (right arm on top) in front of the chest, start movement with whole strength of body as soon as feet are fixed.
4:South

1 挙動

【❺を西から見る】

❺seen from west.

足の動作●❸のまま。
立ち方●❸のまま。
手の動作●左中段外受け（下位）をする。右拳は胸側（下位）に引く。

着眼点●南

留意点●1〜16挙動は、全身均等に満身の力で、柔らかになめらかに静かに動作する。脇の締めが緩み、肘が体より離れて上下に動くことと、反対の引き手が不十分にならないこと。

1:Same as in ❸
2:Left-Seishandachi
3:Left-Chudan-Sotouke(lower position).Pull back right fist to right side of body.
4:South

Point: Motion 1-16 must be done with all strength spreading over whole body evenly and with smooth and quiet movement. Take care neither loosen underarm, nor to move elbows up and down apart from the body,nor to be incomplete of pulling the hands.

2 挙動

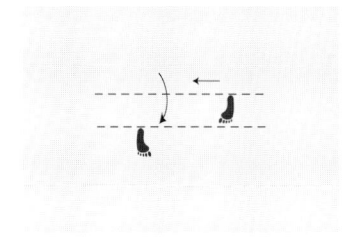

❼ ❽ ❾

足の動作●❸のまま。
立ち方●❸のまま。
手の動作●右拳中段突き（下位）をする。左拳は胸側（下位）に引く。

着眼点●南

足の動作●左踵をやや内転し、右足を内側より弧を描きながら南に進める。
立ち方●右セイシャン立ち。
手の動作●右拳を左下腹前に運び、右前膊を返しながら。

備考●足の運びは「セイシャン」の進み方を参照。以下同じ。

着眼点●南

留意点●移動のとき前足の爪先が外に向かないように。

1:Same as in ❸
2:Left-Seishandachi
3:Right-Chudantsuki (lower position). Pull back left fist to left side of boday.
4:South

1:While turning left heel slightly inward, advance right foot toward south as if drawing a circle from inside.
2:Right-Seishandachi
3:While turning wrist, pull right fist in front of left abdomen. Left fist remains the same.
4:South

Note:As for feet movements refer to "Feet of Seishan".

Point:In movement, pay attention not to turn front foot toe outside.

セイシャン

3挙動　　4挙動　　5挙動

❿　　❶　　⓬

足の動作●❽のまま。
立ち方●❽のまま。
手の動作●右中段外受け（下位）をする。左拳は胸側に引いたまま。

備考●1挙動❺の左右反対の形。

着眼点●南

足の動作●❽のまま。
立ち方●❽のまま。
手の動作●左拳中段突き（下位）をする。右拳は胸側（下位）に引く。

備考●2挙動の左右反対動作。

着眼点●南

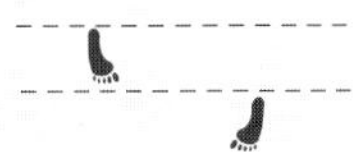

足の動作●左足を南に進め、1挙動の立ち方となる。
立ち方●左セイシャン立ち。
手の動作●左中段外受け（下位）をする。右拳は引いたまま。

備考●3挙動の左右反対動作。

着眼点●南

1:Same as in ❽
2:Right-Seishandachi
3:Right-Chudan-Sotouke (lower position). Left fist remains the same.
4:South

Note:Reverse of ❺.

1:Same as in ❽
2:Right Seishandachi.
3:Left-Chudantsuki(lower position).Pull back right fist to right side of the body.
4:South

Note:Reverse of ❼.

1:Advance left foot toward south.
2:Left-Seishandachi.
3:Left-Chudan-Sotouke(lower position).Right fist remains the same.
4:South

Note:Same as in ❿(left and right is riversed).

▶セイシャン篇　169

6 挙動

⑬

足の動作●⑫のまま。
立ち方●⑫のまま。
手の動作●右拳中段突き（下位）をする。左拳は胸側（下位）に引く。

備考●2挙動に同じ。

着眼点●南

1:Same as in ⑫
2:Left-Seishandachi
3:Right-Chudantsuki(lower position).Pull back left fist to left side of the body.
4:South

Note:Same as in ❼.

7 挙動

⑭

足の動作●⑫のまま。
立ち方●⑫のまま。
手の動作●両拳を人差指一本拳（コーサー）にして、胸の中央部、乳のすこし上のところに運び（両拳先はわずかに離す）。

着眼点●南

1:Same as in ⑫
2:Left-Seishandachi
3:Both fists to Hitosashiyubi (forefinger)Ipponken(Kohsah), hold them in front of upper part of chest(tips of both fists slightly apart).
4:South

⑮

足の動作●⑫のまま。
立ち方●⑫のまま。
手の動作●両肘を挙上する。

留意点●肘受けの基礎動作。肘上げは手首を曲げてはならない。

着眼点●南

1:Same as in ⑫
2:Left-Seishandachi
3:Lift both elbows up.
4:South

Point:Basic motion of Hijiuke. Don't bend wrists at Hijiage.

セイシャン

8 挙動

⑯　⑰　⑱

足の動作●⓬のまま。
立ち方●⓬のまま。
手の動作●人差指一本拳（コーサー）のまま、左右同時に中段突き（下位）をする。

留意点●肘を絞り込みながら手首を曲げないで突き下す。

着眼点●南

1: Same as in ⓬
2: Left-Seishandachi.
3: With Hitosashiyubi-Ipponken (kohsah), Chudantsuki (lower position) with both fists at the same time.
4: South

Point: Squeezing both elbows, Tsukioroshi without bending wrists.

足の動作●⓬のまま。
立ち方●⓬のまま。
手の動作●両手を手刀にし、両前膊撓骨側で上段払い受けを、前方より。

着眼点●南

1: Same as in ⓬.
2: Left-Seishandachi.
3: Change both fists to Shuto and execute Jyodan-Haraiuke with radius.
4: South

挙動の分解7　Seishan Kumite in detail

①

9挙動　　　　　　　　　　　　　　　　10挙動

❶⑲　　　　　　　❷⑳　　　　　　　　❸㉑

足の動作●⓬のまま。
立ち方●⓬のまま。
手の動作●両側方に左右同時に行なう（両掌面は向き合う）。

着眼点●南

1:Same as in ⓬
2:Left-Seishandachi.
3:Left both hands up at the same time with palms facing each other.
4:South

足の動作●⓬のまま。
立ち方●⓬のまま。
手の動作●両手刀の前膊尺骨側で、押し下げるように両側方に同時に下段手刀払いをする。

着眼点●南

1:Same as in ⓬
2:Left-Seishandachi.
3:Gedanbarai with ulna parts of both Shuto at the same time as if pushing downward to both side of the body.
4:South

留意点●肘を少し押し出しながら力点を手首の方に移し切り下げる。肘が止まって手首の方が先に動かないように。

Point:Pushing out both ellows a little, move power point toward wrists. Wrists must not move while elbows are left unmoved.

挙動の分解9、10　Seishan Kumite in detail

②　　　　　　　③　　　　　　　④

セイシャン

11挙動

㉒  ㉓  ㉔

下段写真㉕へ

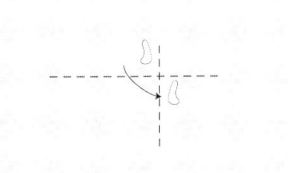

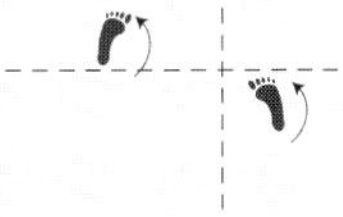

足の動作●左足を軸とし、右足を南東に運ぶ。
立ち方●右足を前に両脚を交差する。
手の動作●両手刀は胸前で交差し（右掌面下向きで下側、左掌面上向きで上側）。

着眼点●南

留意点●膝を柔らかく使い、重心移動を正確に行なう。腰が曲がったり、中心軸が大きくぶれたりしないこと。中段、下段の受けを同時に行なう。下段の肘が体側外に出るのは肘が浮き受けが弱くなる。

足の動作●体を左に回転させ、両足先は北に向く。
立ち方●左セイシャン立ち。
手の動作●左手刀下段払い。右手刀は掌面上向きに橈骨側で中段外受けをする（右手首をわずかに背屈する）。

着眼点●北

1: Pivoting on the left foot, step right foot toward southeast.
2: Cross both legs with right foot in front.
3: Cross both arms in front of chest with left hand(palm facing upward)on top of right hand(palm facing downward)
4: South

Point: Using both knees flexibly, gravity movement should be done precisely. Waist must not bend or central axis of the body must not move a lot.
Execute Chudan-Uke and Gedan-Uke at the same time. In case Gedan elbow comes out of the body, the elbow loosens and weakens defense.

1: Turn body to left and both toes point north.
2: Left-Seishandachi
3: Gedanbarai with Left-Shuto-Chudan-Sotouke with radius side of Right-Shuto with palm facing upward (twist right wrist slightly backward).
4: North

㉕ ㉔の形が極まる途中を北から見る Process of finishing ㉔ seen from north

㉖ ㉔を北から見る ㉔ seen from north.

㉗ ㉔を東から見る ㉔ seen from east.

▶セイシャン篇 173

12挙動

㉘

【12挙動は、北から見た写真で説明する】

留意点●手首をわずかに撓骨側に外屈し、相手の突きを払い受けて懸ける気持。
引手は体側より、離さず、手首のみ外稔させながら背手、手刀の順で斜め下後方に引く。

Motion 12 will be explained as seen from north.

Point: Twist right wrist outward as if hooking opponent's Tsuki with Haraiuke.
Pull back right arm diagonally in the order of Haishu and Shuto, twisting wrist only outside without parting from body.

㉙

【㉘を北から見る】
足の動作●㉔のまま。
立ち方●㉔のまま。
手の動作●右腕を後方に引きつつ、手首を背屈させたまま掌面を返し。

着眼点●北

㉘seen from noth

1: Same as in ㉔.
2: Left-Seishandachi
3: While turning around right palm, pull back right arm keeping wrist bent backward.
4: North

㉚

【㉘を北から見る】
足の動作●㉔のまま。
立ち方●㉔のまま。
手の動作●右手を胸側下方に引く（懸けた手で、相手の手首を握って引く気持ち）。左手はそのまま。

着眼点●北

㉘seen from noth

1: Same as in ㉔.
2: Left-Seishandachi
3: Pull back right hand to right side of body(as if grabbing and pulling opponent's wrist with hooking hand). Left hand remains the same.
4: North

挙動の分解11、12　Seishan Kumite in detail

⑤　⑥　⑦

13挙動	14挙動	セイシャン 15挙動
㉛	㉜	㉝

| 足の動作●右足を北に進める。
立ち方●右セイシャン立ち。
手の動作●右手刀下段払い、左（手刀撓骨側）中段外受けをする。

備考●㉘の左右反対の形。

着眼点●北

1:Advance right foot toward north.
2:Right-Seishandachi
3:Gedanbarai with Right-Shuto. Chudan-Sotouke with radius side of Left-Shuto.
4:North

Note:Right and left side is reversed with㉘ | 足の動作●㉛のまま。
立ち方●㉛のまま。
手の動作●左手掌を返しながら胸側下方に引く。右手そのまま。

備考●㉘の左右反対の形。

着眼点●北

1:Same as in ㉛
2:Right-Seishandachi
3:While turning around left palm,pull back left hand to left side of body.Right hand remains same.
4:North

Note:Right and left side is reversed with㉘ | 足の動作●左足を北に進める。
立ち方●左セイシャン立ち。
手の動作●左手刀下段払い、右（手刀撓骨側）中段外受けをする。

備考●11挙動㉔に同じ

着眼点●北

1:Advance left foot toward north.
2:Left-Seishandachi
3:Gedanbarai with Left-Shuto. Chudan-sotouke with radius side of Right-Shuto.
4:North

Note:Same as in ㉔ |

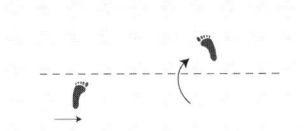

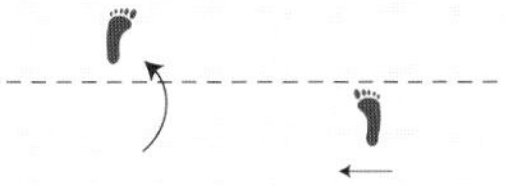

⑤、⑥、⑦の手の動きをクローズアップしてみる。　　　　　　　　　　Close-up of ⑤,⑥ and ⑦

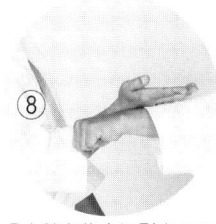

⑧右腕を後方に引きつつ、手首を十分背屈しながら手掌を返し、
Pulling right arm backward,turn around palm with wrist bending backward.

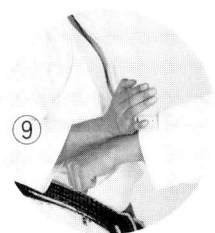

⑨右手刀の掌面が平らになる程度に手首を背屈し、さらに撓骨側にわずかに外屈しながら、払い受けをする。
Bend wrist backward so that palm of Right-Shuto becomes horizontal. Then turning it slightly outward toward radius side, execute Haraiuke.

⑩相手の手首を親指と薬指、小指で握って引く（他の指は自然に添える）。
Grab and pull opponent's left wrist with thumb,ring finger and little finger(other fingers placed naturally).

16挙動　　17挙動

㉞　㉟　㊱

足の動作●㉝のまま。
立ち方●㉝のまま。
手の動作●右手拳を返しながら、胸側下方に引く。左手そのまま。

留意点●12挙動㉘に同じ。上段払い受けを腕の力だけで受けたり、前屈立ちにならないようにし、後ろ足の踵が浮いたり外側に流れて動いてはならない。

着眼点●北

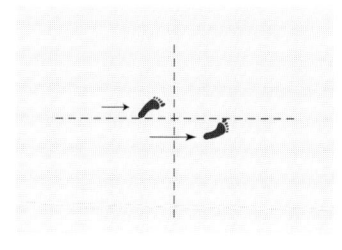

足の動作●右足を東に寄り足で進む。
立ち方●右縦セイシャン立ち（右足拇指先と左踵の内側が同一線上になる）。
手の動作●右拳上段外受け、左拳は胸側に引く。

着眼点●東

足の動作●㉟のまま。
立ち方●㉟のまま。
手の動作●左、右と連続中段突きをする。引き手はそれぞれ胸側に引く。

備考●17、18挙動は連続して行なう。

着眼点●東

1:Same as in ㉝
2:Left-Seishandachi
3:While turning around right fist,pull back right hand to right side of body.Left hand remains the same.
4:North

1:Take right foot leaping step toward east.Left foot following in yoriashi.
2:Right-Tate-Seishandachi(tip of right foot's big toe should be on the line of inside of left heel).
3:Jyodan-Soto-Uke with right fist. Pull back left fist to left side of the body.
4:East

1:Same as in ㉟
2:Right-Tate-Seishandachi
3:Repeat Chudantsuki with left and then right fist.Pull back each Hikite to each side of the body.
4:East

Note:Motion of 17 and 18 should be a continuous movement.

Point:Same as in ㉘. Don't defense only with arm strength, nor by Zenkutsudachi, nor with up left heel. Don't move away outside.

セイシャン

18挙動

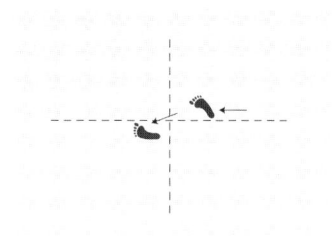

足の動作●体を180°左回りで、左足を西に躍進し、右足を寄り足で進める。
立ち方●左縦セイシャン立ち。
手の動作●左拳上段外受け、右拳は胸側に引く。

着眼点●西

1: Turn body 180° to left and take left foot leaping step toward west. Right foot follows in Tsugiashi.
2: Left-Tate-Seishandachi
3: Jyodan-Sotouke with left fist. Pull back right fist to right side of the body.
4: West

19挙動

【**足の動作**●㊳のまま。
立ち方●㊳のまま。
手の動作●右、左と連続中段突きをする。引き手はそれぞれ胸側に引く。

備考●19、20挙動は連続して行なう（17、18挙動の左右反対となる）。

着眼点●西

1: Same as in ㊳
2: Left-Tate-Seishandachi
3: Repeat Chudantsuki with right and then left fist. Pull back each Hikite to each side of the body.
4: West

Note: Motion 19 and 20 should be a continuous movement.(Reverse of motion 17 and 18.)

▶セイシャン篇

20挙動　21挙動

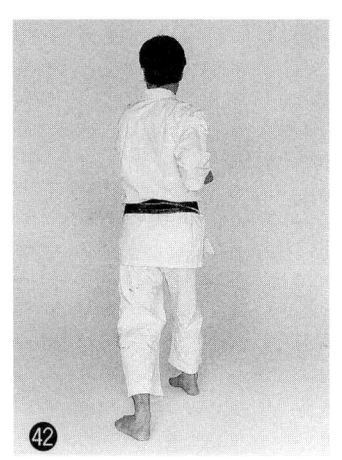

⑳

㊶

㊷

足の動作●体を90°右転し、右足前を北に寄り足で進む。
立ち方●右縦セイシャン立ち。
手の動作●右拳上段外受け。左拳は胸側に引く。

着眼点●北

足の動作●㊶のまま。
立ち方●㊶のまま。
手の動作●左、右と連続中段突きをする。引き手はそれぞれ胸側に引く。

備考●21、22挙動は連続して行なう（17、18挙動に同じ）。

着眼点●北

1: Turn body 90° to right, then take right foot leaping step(Yoriashi) toward north.
2: Right-Tate-Seishandachi
3: Jyodan-Sotouke with right fist. Pull back left fist to left side of the body.
4: North

1: Same as in ㊶
2: Right-Tate-Seishandachi
3: Repeat Chudantsuki with left and then right fist. Pull back each Hikite to each side of the body.
4: North

Note: Motion 21 and 22 should be done continuously, and same as in motion 17 and 18.

22挙動

⑬ ⑭ ⑮

【⑭を北から見る】

⑭seen from north.

足の動作●後方からの踏込みに対し、左足を引いてかわすと同時に、前方に対し前蹴りの姿勢をとる。
立ち方●右片足で立つ。
手の動作●前蹴りの姿勢をとると同時に、左裏拳で相手の鼻を掬いあげ、右拳は胸側に引く。

着眼点●北

1: While lifting left knee to dodge Fumi-komi from behind, take stance for Maegeri.
2: Stand on right foot.
3: While taking stance for Maegeri, scoop opponent's nose upward with Left-Uraken. Pull back right fist to right side of the body.
4: North

挙動の分解23　Seishan Kumite in detail

⑪ ⑫ ⑬ ⑭

23挙動

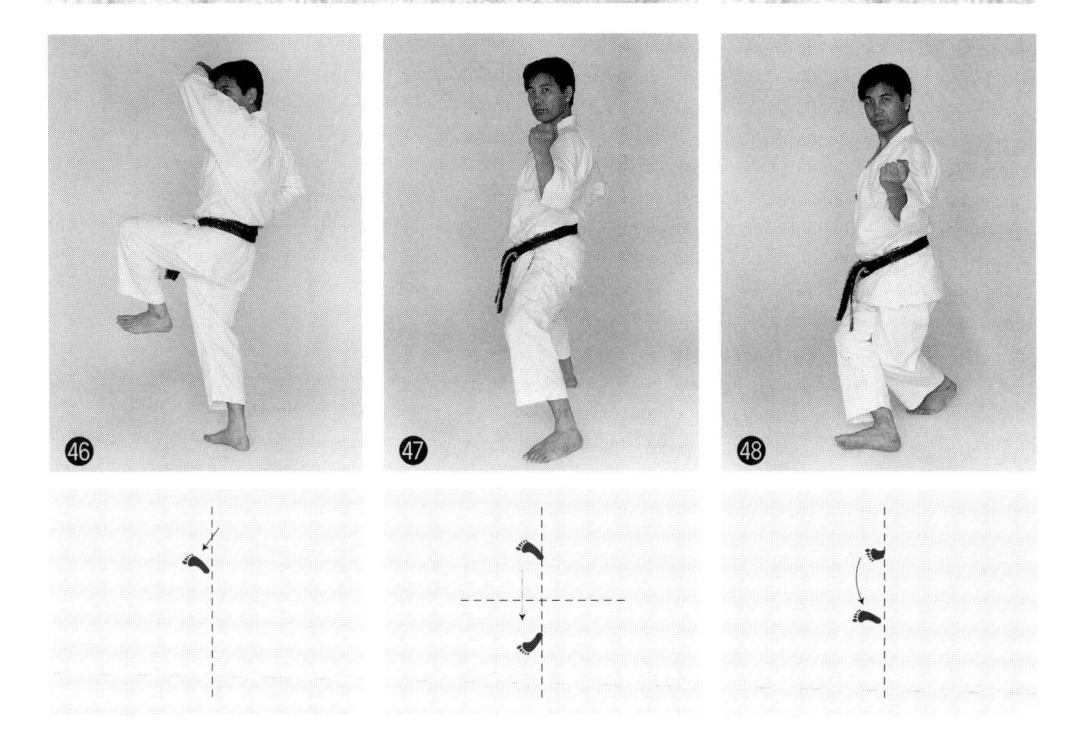

足の動作●体を左に回転させ、足先は北西を向く。
立ち方●右片足で立つ。
手の動作●掬いあげた左拳をそのまま頭上に構えながら。

留意点●掬い打ちをした後惰性で後ろを振り向いてはならない。打ちあげた腕の力が抜けないまま踏み込み、裏打ちを行なうと何れも弱くなり立ち方も不安定となる。

足の動作●左足を南に踏み込む。
立ち方●四股立ち。
手の動作●左裏拳を上より下に打ちおろす。右拳は胸側に構えたまま。

足の動作●右足を左足の前に千鳥に交差させて、南に踏み出す。
立ち方●右足を前に両脚を交差して立つ。
手の動作●両拳はそのままに、左腕を相手に掴まれ引かれるにまかせて体を送り。

着眼点●南

1: Turn body to left, tips pointing toward northwest.
2: Stand on right foot.
3: Hold scooped up left fist above head. Right fist remains the same.

1: Step in left foot toward south.
2: Shikodachi
3: Strike left Uraken downward. Right fist remains the same.

1: Step right foot toward south and cross with left foot in Chidori.
2: Stand with feet crossed with right foot in front.
3: Both fists remain the same. Step out close to opponent by force of grasping left arm and pulling by him.
4: South

Point: After executing Sukiuchi, never turn around by force of mere habit. If Fumikomi and Urauchi are executed without removing arm strength both Fumikomi and Urauchi debiliate original strengh and will be instable at Tachikata.

セイシャン

24挙動

⓴⓴ ⓰⓰ ⓱⓱

【㊿を西から見る】
㊿seen from west.

足の動作●右足で立ち、左横蹴りをする。
立ち方●右片足立ち。
手の動作●左横蹴りと同時に、左拳を強く胸側に引く。右拳はそのまま。

足の動作●蹴った左足を突込みの足におろす。
立ち方●順突きの突込みの足（左前屈立ち、Ｔ字形）。
手の動作●左拳で下段に突っ込む。右拳は構えたまま。

留意点●体の移動は腰を曲げたり、上下動かさない。左拳の引きと蹴りは同時に行なうが、引足が不十分だと後ろ足の膝や腰が曲がり下段突きが弱くなる。

着眼点●南   着眼点●南

1:Left-Yokogeri standing right foot.
2:Standing on right foot.
3:While executing Left-Yokogeri, pull back left fist forcefully to left side of the body. Right fist remains the same.
4:South

1:Put down left foot to become Tsukikomiashi.
2:Tsukikomiashi for Juntsuki (Left-Zenkutsudachi in T-shape).
3:Thrust left fist toward Gedan. Right fist remains the same.
4:South

Point:Waist must not bend nor move up and down in movement. Pulling back left fist and kick are executed at the same time. However, if pulling back foot is insufficient, back foot knee and waist will bend and Gedantsuki will weaken.

▶セイシャン篇

25挙動

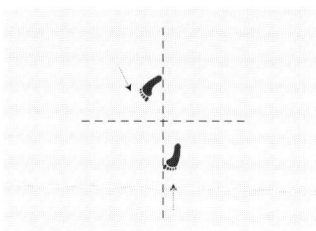

㊷

足の動作●右足を軸に、腰を左にひねり、内輪に立つ。
立ち方●左縦セイシャン立ち。
手の動作●右中段逆突き、左拳は胸側に引く。

着眼点●南

1: Pivoting on right foot, twist hips to left and turn toes inward.
2: Left-Tate-Seishandachi.
3: Chudan-Gyakutsuki with right fist. Pull back left fist to left side of the body.
4: South

26挙動

㊷

足の動作●㊷のまま。
立ち方●㊷のまま。
手の動作●左拳上段揚げ受け。右拳は胸側に引く。

着眼点●南

1: Same as in ㊷
2: Left-Tate-Seishandachi.
3: Jyodan-Ageuke with left fist. Pull back right fist to right side of the body.
4: South

㊸

足の動作●右足を引いて前蹴りの姿勢をとる。
立ち方●左片足で立つ。
手の動作●右裏拳で前方の相手の鼻を掬いあげ、そのまま頭上に構えながら、左拳は胸側に引く。

備考●23挙動を右で行なう。

着眼点●南

1: Lift right knee and take stance for Maegeri.
2: Stand on left foot.
3: While scooping upward opponent's nose with Right-Uraken and holding it above head, pull back left fist to left side of the body.
4: South

Note: Reverse of motion 23.

挙動の分解24〜26　Seishan Kumite in detail

⑮　⑯　⑰　⑱

セイシャン

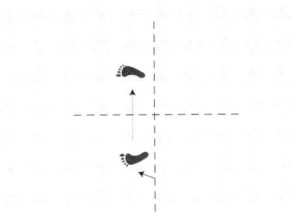

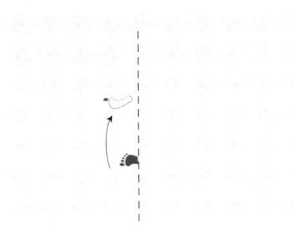

27挙動

足の動作●体を右転し、右足を北に踏み込む。
立ち方●四股立ち。
手の動作●右裏拳で打ちおろし、左拳は引いたまま。

1: Turn body to right and step right foot into north.
2: Shikodachi
3: Strike Right-Uraken downward. Left fist remains the same.

足の動作●左足を右足の前に交差させ、北に踏み出す。
立ち方●左足を前に、両脚を交差して立つ。
手の動作●両拳はそのまま。

備考●24挙動を左右反対に行なう。

着眼点●北

1: Step left foot toward north and cross with right foot.
2: Feet crossed to stand with left foot in front.
3: Both fists remains the same.
4: North
Note: Reverse of motion 24.

足の動作●左足で立ち、右横蹴りをする。
立ち方●左片足で立つ。
手の動作●蹴ると同時に、右拳は胸側に強く引く。左拳はそのまま。

1: Stand on left foot and execute Right-Yokogeri.
2: Standing on left foot.
3: While executing Right-Yokogeri, pull back right fist forcefully to right side of body. Left fist remains the same.

28挙動

(58)

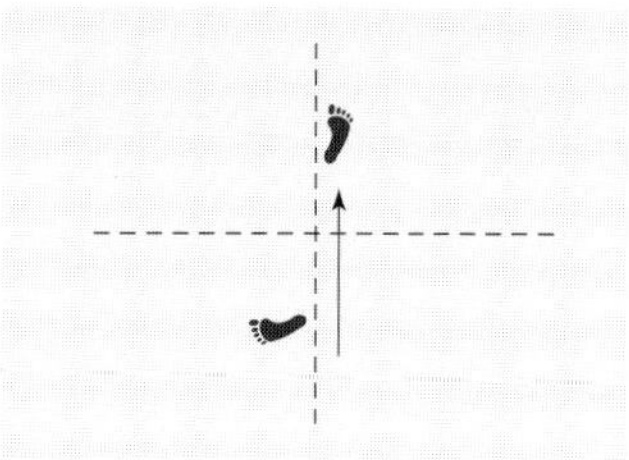

足の動作●右足を北に突込みの足でおろす。
立ち方●順突きの突込み（右前屈立ち、T字形）。
手の動作●右拳で下段に突込む。左拳は引いたまま。

着眼点●北

1:Put down right foot toward north to become Tsukikomiashi
2:Tsukikomiashi for Juntsuki (Right-Zenkutsudachi in T-shape)
3:Thrust right fist toward Gedan. Left fist remains the same.
4:North

29挙動

(59)

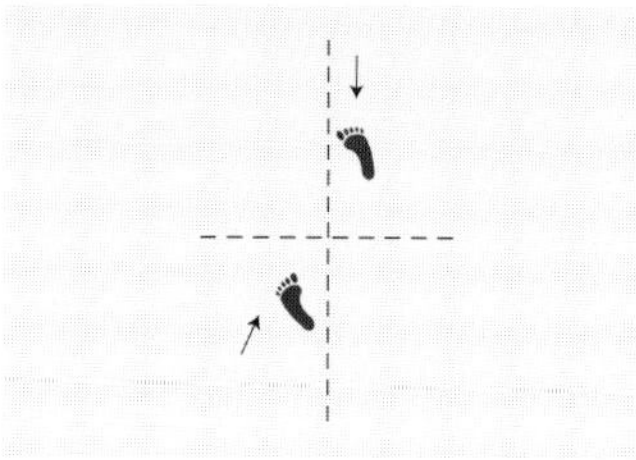

足の動作●左足を軸に、腰を右にひねり内輪に立つ。
立ち方●右縦セイシャン立ち。
手の動作●左中段逆突き、右拳は胸側に引く。

留意点●下段の突込みから逆突（縦セイシャン立ち）になるが、そのとき腰を高くしてはならない。

着眼点●北

1:With left foot as axis, twist hips to right and turn toes inward.
2:Right-Tate-Seishandachi
3:Chudan-Gyakutsuki with left fist. Pull back right fist to right side of the body.
4:North

Point: While movement proceeds from Tsukkomi of Gedan to Gyakutsuki(Tate-Seishandachi), never make waist position high.

30挙動

(60)

足の動作●(59)のまま。
立ち方●(59)のまま。
手の動作●右拳上段揚げ受け、左拳は胸側に引く。

着眼点●北

1:Same as in (59)
2:Right-Tate-Seishandachi
3:Jyodan-Ageuke with right fist.Pull back left fist to left side of the body.
4:North

セイシャン

31挙動

⑥1　⑥2　⑥3

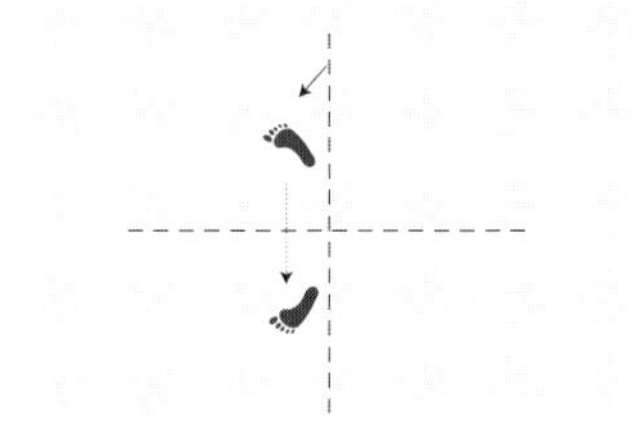

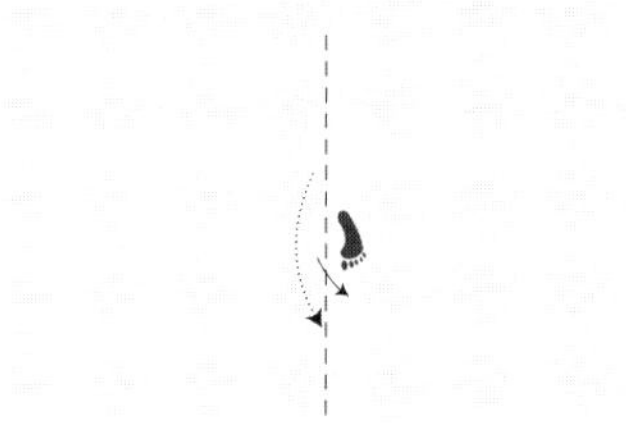

足の動作●左足を引きあげて前蹴りの姿勢をとる。
立ち方●右片足で立つ。
手の動作●左裏拳を上段に掬いあげ、そのまま頭上に構えながら、右拳は胸側に引く。

留意点●23挙動に同じ。

着眼点●北

1: Lift left knee and take stance for Maegeri.
2: Stand on right foot.
3: While scooping upward opponent's nose with Left-Uraken and holding it above head, pull back right fist to side of the body.
4: North

Point: Same as in motion 23

足の動作●体を左に回転し、左足を南に踏む込む。
立ち方●四股立ち。
手の動作●左裏拳を上より打ちおろす。右拳は引いたまま。

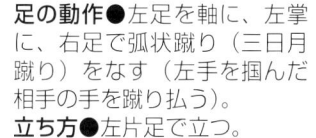

1: Turn body to left and step in left foot toward south
2: Shikodachi
3: Strike Left-Uraken downward. Right fist remains the same.

足の動作●左足を軸に、左掌に、右足で弧状蹴り（三日月蹴り）をなす（左手を掴んだ相手の手を蹴り払う）。
立ち方●左片足で立つ。
手の動作●左手は開き、右蹴り足をあてる。右拳は胸側に引いたまま。

着眼点●南

1: Kojyogeri (Mikazukigeri) against left palm with right foot (kick away opponent's hand grabbing your left hand).
2: Stand on left foot.
3: Open left hand and kick against left palm with right foot. Right fist remains the same.
4: South

挙動の分解31、32　Seishan Kumite in detail

㉑　㉒　㉓

32挙動

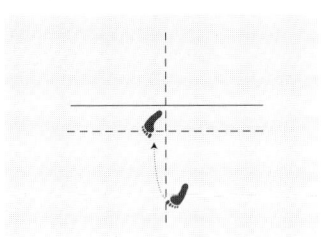

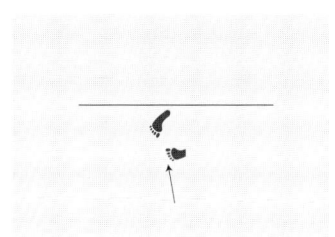

⑥⑷

足の動作●蹴った右足を北に引き、内輪に立つ。
立ち方●左縦セイシャン立ち。
手の動作●右中段逆突き、左拳は胸側に引く。

留意点●三日月蹴りは腰の回転で行なう。足だけ回して左手を下げて当ててはならない。

着眼点●南

1:Pull down right foot backward to north and turn toes inward.
2:Left-Tate-Seishandachi
3:Chudan-Gyakutsuki with right fist. Pull back left fist to left side of body.
4:South

Point:Mikazukigeri is performed by waist turn.Hitting by turning foot only with hanging down left hand should not be done.

⑥⑸

足の動作●左足を爪先立ちにして右足前に引きつけ、腰をやや右にひねって急所をかばう。
立ち方●右足はそのままに、左足爪先立ちで引きつける。
手の動作●両手を猫手（五指を十分内屈させる）にして、両手首を背屈させて両胸側に引きながら。

1:With tiptoeing left foot,pull it in front of right foot and protect groin by twisting hips to right.
2:Staying right foot the same,pull left foot in tiptoeing.
3:Both hands become Nekote (bend all fingers as much as possible inside of palms). Bend both wrists backward and pull back hands under both armpits.

33挙動

⑥⑹

足の動作●⑥⑸のまま。
立ち方●⑥⑸のまま。
手の動作●体をやや落すと同時に両掌底を突きおろして、下段受けをする（両手首の内側が接する）。

留意点●掌底受けはゆっくり行なわない。引きつけた左足は膝を締め爪先を内に踵を外にする様に立つ。

1:Same as in ⑥⑸
2:Same as in ⑥⑸
3:While lowering body slightly, execute Gedanuke by thrusting both Shotei downward (both wrists touching on inside)

Point:Don't execute Shoteiuke slowly. Draw left foot to tight knee and stand with turning toe tips inside and heel outside.

止め

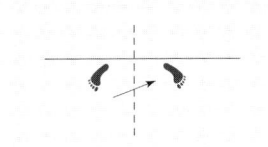

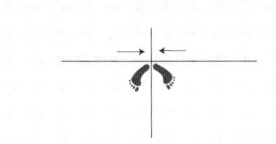

❻❼

足の動作●右足を軸に、左足を引いて用意の姿勢にもどる。
立ち方●八字立ち。
手の動作●両手を用意の構えにもどす。

留意点●止め、直れの場合も残心に注意する。

着眼点●南

1:Pivoting on right foot,pull back left foot and return to Yo-i posture.
2:Hachijidachi
3:Return both hands to Yo-i position.
4:South

Point:Pay attention on Zanshin (a state of alertness) at Yame and Naore.

直立

❻❽

足の動作●足を左、右と引き、結び立ちに直る。
立ち方●結び立ち。
手の動作●両手は開いて大腿部前に軽く垂れる。

着眼点●南

1:Pulling left foot then right foot, return to Musubidachi.
2:Musubidachi
3:Open both hands and place them lightly in front of thighs.
4:South

挙動の分解33　Seishan Kumite in detail

㉔　㉕

チントウ篇

特徴

軽快かつ敏捷な形で、立ち方の種類も多く、その立ち方の変化は即ち体位の変化を表している。従って「緩急」「力の強弱」「重心の安定」が特に要求される形の一つである。

CHINTO is a nimble and agile KATA having various types of stance and its alteration signifies a variety of posture. Consequently, CHINTO is one of the types required to exhibit "quick and slow motion", "strength and weakness of power" and "balance of gravity".

チントウの立ち方

①（用意の姿勢から）右足を左足の後方に引き、両足先はほぼ南西を向き、前後の足幅は軽い四股立ち程度。
②体をすこし落とし、両脚をごくわずかに内輪にして立つ。ほぼ真半身になる。

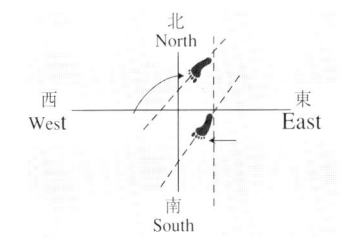

Stance of CHINTO

①(from posture yo-i) Pull right foot toward back of left foot with both toes pointing almost southwest. Width between feet is about that of narrow Shikodachi.
②Lower body slightly, bend both legs slightly inward to be almost Ma-hanmi.

CHINTO

直立　　　　　用意　　　　　1挙動

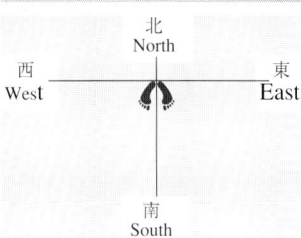

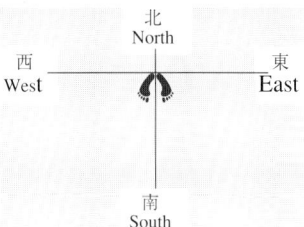

足の動作●結び立ち。
立ち方●結び立ち。
手の動作●両手は開いて、大腿部前に軽く垂れる。

着眼点●南

Remarks
1:Feet
2:Stance
3:Hands
4:Point to see

1:Musubidachi
2:Musubidachi
3:Open both hands and hang them down lightly in front of thighs.
4:South

挙動の分解1〜4　　Chinto Kumite in detail

注1.形では1、2の左右の払い受けを同時に行う。

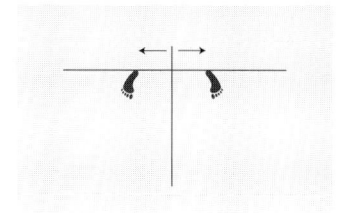

足の動作●結び立ちより足を左、右と開き、八字立ちとなる（両踵の間隔は1足長半）。
立ち方●八字立ち。
手の動作●両手は大腿部前で軽く握る。

着眼点●南

1:Open left foot, then right foot from Musubidachi.Then, Hachijidachi (Width between heels is a foot and half apart).
2:Hachijidachi
3:Grip both hands lightly in front of thighs.
4:South

<Note 1> In Kata, execute right (1) and left (2) Haraiuke at the same time.

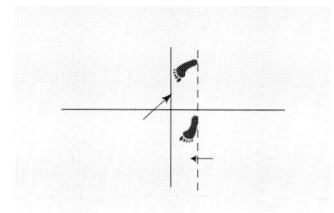

足の動作●右足を北（左足の後ろ）に引き、両足先を南西に向け、体はほぼ真半身にする。
立ち方●両踵は縦一線上にあり、両脚をやや内輪にする。歩幅は軽い四股立ち程度とする。
手の動作●右手掌、左手背面で同時に上段払い受けをする（右手が内側となり、両手首付近で交差する）。
留意点●両手を同時に動作するが、左右べつべつの受けの動作を同時にするのである。

着眼点●南

1:Pull back right foot toward north(back of left foot) with both feet pointing southwest. Almost ma-hanmi
2:With both heels on a straight line, bend legs slightly inward.Width between feet is about that of narrow shikodachi.
3:Execute Jyodan-Haraiuke with right palm and back of left hand at the same time(cross both hands at about wrists with right hand inside).
4:South

Point:Move both hands at the same time, while each hand executes different Uke motion.

2挙動　　3挙動　　4挙動　　チントウ

❹　　❺　　❻

❹
足の動作●❸のまま。
立ち方●❸のまま。
手の動作●両手で同時に中段打ち落しをする（左手が上で掌面下向き、右手下で掌面上向き）。
留意点●❹の中段落し受けは右腕が水平に左脇腹方向へ受ける。
❻の腰の回転が充分な突きで縦セイシャン立ちを正確に。
❸～❻は連続技として評価する。

1:Same as in ❸.
2:Same as in ❸.
3:Execute Chudan-Uchiotoshi by both hands at the same time with left hand (palm facing downward) on right hand (palm facing upward).

Point:
❹.Chudan-Otoshiuke is to defend toward left side of the body by horizontal right arm.
❻. Tsuki with an adequate hips turn and Tate-Seishandachi precisely.
❸～❻ All performances will be judged as a continuous technique.

❺
足の動作●❸のまま。
立ち方●❸のまま。
手の動作●左拳中段突きをし、右拳は胸側に引く。
着眼点●南

1:Same as in ❸.
2:Same as in ❸.
3:Execute Chudantsuki with left fist and pull back right fist to right side of body.
4:South

❻
足の動作●右足を軸に、腰を左にひねって縦セイシャンの足になり、内輪に立つ。
立ち方●左縦セイシャン立ち。
手の動作●右拳中段逆突きをし、左拳は胸側に引く。
備考●1～4挙動まで連続して行う。

着眼点●南

1:Pivoting on right foot, twist body toward left to become Tate-Seishan feet with toes pointing inward.
2:Left-Tate-Seishandachi
3:Execute Chudan-Gyakutsuki with right fist and pull back left fist to left side of body.
4:South
Note:Motion 1－4 must be executed in a continuous movememt.

---

③ 右手刀の甲面側前膊で左脇を打ち落し受けをする。
Block his further Left-Chudan-Tsuki by Uchiotoshi with wrist part of back of Right-Shuto.

④ （その場で）相手の中段突きを左掌面側の前膊で打ち落し受けをする。
(in the same position) Block his Right-Chudantsuki by Uchiotoshi with wrist part of left palm.

⑤ 注2.形では3、4の受けの動作を左右同時に行う。
注3.受け、または払いを行なった後、ただちに攻め（突き、または蹴り等）をするのが原則であるが、形においては受け、払いののちの攻めを省略する場合が多い。

⑥ <Note 2> In Kata, execute right (3) and left(4) Uke at the same time.
<Note 3> Generally, it is the rule to counter-attack (with Tsuki, Keri, etc.) immediately after Uke or Harai. However, in Kata, attacks after Uke or Harai are apt to be omitted.

5 挙動

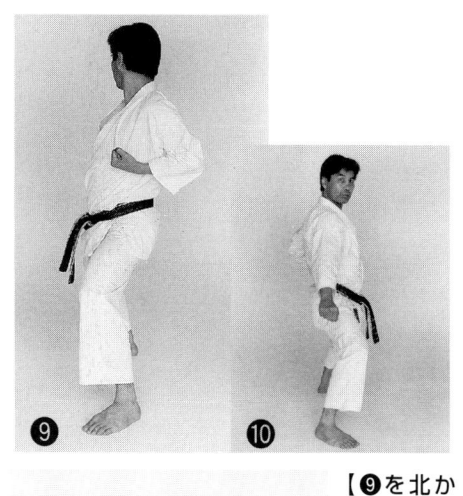

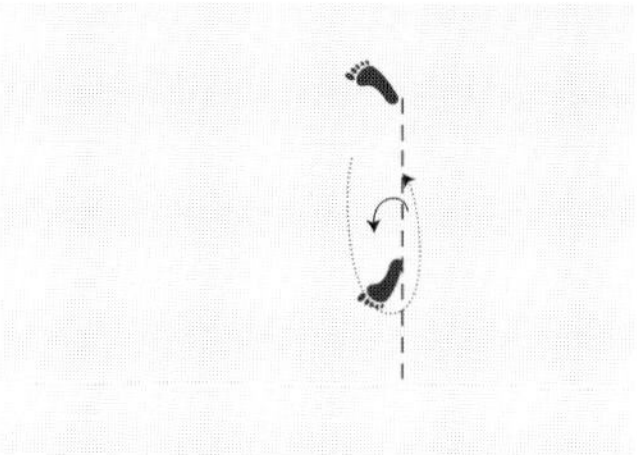

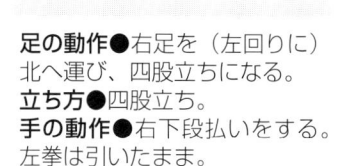

【❾を北から見る】

❾seen from north.

足の動作●後ろからの蹴込みに対し、右足を引きあげてはずし（左足を軸とする）、
立ち方●左片足で立つ。
手の動作●右肘を曲げ、右拳は右耳横にあげ、左拳は引いたまま。

着眼点●南

足の動作●右足を左足前に回し、体を左転し、
立ち方●左片足立ち。
手の動作●❼のまま。

着眼点●北

足の動作●右足を（左回りに）北へ運び、四股立ちになる。
立ち方●四股立ち。
手の動作●右下段払いをする。左拳は引いたまま。

着眼点●北

留意点●後足を引き上げたとき、立ち上ったり、流し受けの肘を高くあげたりしてはならない。
回るとき中心軸がぶれないこと。

1:Against kick from behind, lift right foot to dodge it (put weight on left foot).
2:Stand on left foot.
3:Bending right elbow, lift right fist beside right ear, while holding left fist in the same position.
4:South

1:Bring right foot in front of left foot and turn body to left.
2:Stand on left foot.
3:Same as in 7.
4:North

1:Turn body to left and put down left foot toward north, then, Shikodachi.
2:Shikodachi
3:Right-Gedanbarai.Left fist remains the same.
4:North

Point:When back foot is raised, don't stand up nor raise high Nagashiuke elbow.When the body turns, axis must not be blurred.

挙動の分解 5
Chinto Kumite in detail

チントウ

6 挙動

⓫ ⓬

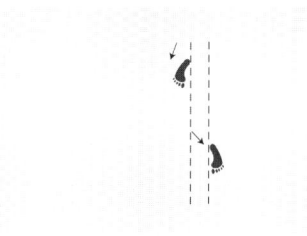

足の動作●右足を軸に、腰を左にひねり南を向き、順突きの足となる。
立ち方●順突きの足（左前屈立ち）。
手の動作●両手刀尺骨側で上段受けをする（右手内側、左手外側に交差する）。

着眼点●南

1: Pivoting on right foot, twist hips to left facing south, then Jyuntsuki feet position.
2: Left-Zenkutsudachi
3: Execute Jyodanuke with ulna sides of both Shuto (cross both arms with right arm inside).
4: South

7 挙動

⓭

足の動作●⓬のまま。
立ち方●⓬のまま。
手の動作●両手刀を正拳にし、尺骨側で左右同時に中段打ち落し受けをする（右拳上、左拳下に交差する）。

1: Same as in ⓬.
2: Left-Zenkustudachi
3: Change both Shuto to Seiken (fist) and execute Chudan-Uchiotoshi with ulna sides of both fists at the same time (cross both arms with right arm on top).

▶チントウ篇 193

8 挙動

⑭

⑮

⑯

足の動作●南へ跳び、二段蹴りの右前蹴りをなし。
立ち方●空中。
手の動作●両拳は両胸前に構えながら。

着眼点●南

足の動作●続いて二段蹴りの左前蹴りをなす。
立ち方●空中。
手の動作●両拳を胸側に引き。

着眼点●南

足の動作●左足を前に、順突きの足にて着地する。
立ち方●順突きの足(左前屈立ち)。
手の動作●左右同時に下段受け(左腕内側、右腕外側に交差)をする。

着眼点●南

1:Jumping toward south, execute Right-Maegeri as first part of Nidangeri.
2:In the air.
3:Hold both fists in front of chest.
4:South

1:Continue Left-Maegeri completing Nidangeri.
2:In the air.
3:Pull back fists to both sides of the body.
4:South

1:Land with left foot in front for Juntsuki feet.
2:Left-Zenkustsudaichi
3:Execute Gedan-Uke with both fists at the same time (cross both arms with left arm indise).
4:South

チントウ

9 挙動

⓱

⓲ 【⓱を北から見る】
⓱seen from north.

⓳

⓴ 【⓳を北から見る】
⓳seen from north.

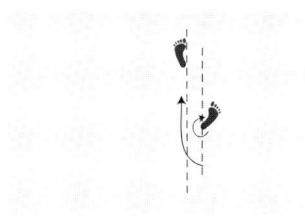

足の動作●右足を軸とし、体を右へ回転させ左足を北に運ぶ。
立ち方●順突きの足（左前屈立ち）。
手の動作●いったん両拳を両胸側に引き。

着眼点●北

足の動作●⓱のまま。
立ち方●⓱のまま。
手の動作●足が極まると同時に、左右下段受け（左腕内側、右腕外側に交差）をする。

着眼点●北

1:Pivoting on right foot, turn body to right and bring left foot to north.
2:Left-Zenkutsudachi
3:Pull back fists to both sides of the body at once.
4:North

1:Same as in ⓱.
2:Left-Zenkutsudachi
3:As soon as setting feet,exectue left and Right-Gedan-Uke (cross both arms with left arm inside).
4:North

▶チントウ篇　195

10挙動

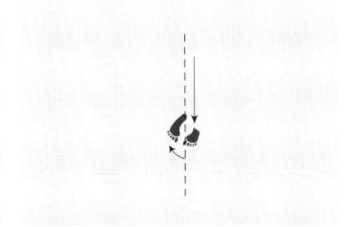

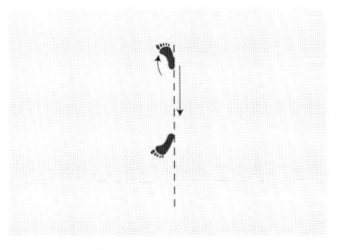

㉑

足の動作●左足を軸とし、体を右転し、左膝をやや曲げ、右脚は伸ばして、体を北に傾倒させる（後ろからの上段突きを引き込み流す動作）。
立ち方●右真半身後屈立ち（右膝を伸ばす）。
手の動作●右拳は下段構え、左拳は胸前に構える。

着眼点●南

1: Pivoting on left foot, turn body to right, then bend left knee slightly and stretch right leg. Lean upper body toward north (as motion for slipping away from Jyodantsuki from behind).
2: Right-Kokutsudachi (stretch right knee) with right ma-hanmi.
3: Gedangamae with right fist. Hold left fist in front of chest.
4: South

㉒

足の動作●右足を軸に、左足を右足に引きつけ、いったん体をまっすぐに起こしながら。
立ち方●右足で立ち、左足を軽く引きつけ、
手の動作●両拳を手刀にし、左手を胸前に構えながら。

着眼点●南

留意点●両拳を手刀にした左右反対の反復練習。一旦立ち上りながら開手で下段の構え（受け）を行なう。

1: While pulling left foot to right foot, raise body straight up at once.
2: Standing on right foot, pull left foot together lightly.
3: Change both fists to Shuto and hold left Shuto in front of chest.
4: South

11挙動

㉓

足の動作●左足を南に進め、体を北に傾倒させる（上段突きを引き込み流す）。
立ち方●左足前の真半身後屈立ち（体は西を向く）。
手の動作●左手刀下段構え。右手刀は胸前に構える。

着眼点●南

1: Step left foot foward to south and lean body toward north (slip away from Jyodantsuki).
2: Left-Kokutsudachi (body faces west) with ma-hanmi.
3: Gedangamae with Left-Shuto. Hold right Shuto in front of chest.
4: South

Point: Change both fists to Shuto and practice with reversed hands repeatedly. While standing up, execute Gedan Kamaeuke with Kaishu.

挙動の分解10、11
Chinto Kumite in detail

⑩

注.下段構えは相手の攻撃を受け払う動作に応用変化できる。

⑪

<Note> Gedangamae would be applied for Ukebarai against opponent's attack.

12挙動　　　チントウ
　　　　　　13挙動

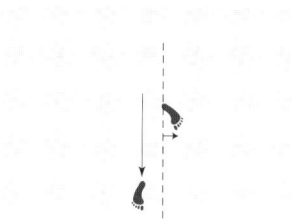

❷④　　　❷⑤　　　❷⑥

足の動作●右足を南に進める（左足を軸とする）。
立ち方●順突きの足（右前屈立ち）。
手の動作●両手は手刀のまま、いったん胸前で交差し（両掌面内向き）。

着眼点●南

留意点●肘を絞って双手受け。肘を広げて上下させたり、肩幅より広く受けないこと。㉖の動作も同じ

1: Step right foot forward to south.
2: Right-Zenkutsudachi
3: While both hands are remaining as Shuto, cross them in front of chest at once with palms facing inside.
4: South

足の動作●㉔のまま。
立ち方●㉔のまま。
手の動作●両手刀とも掌面を外向きに返し、同時に尺骨側上段払い受けをする。

着眼点●南

1: Same as in ㉔.
2: Right-Zenkutsudachi
3: While turning around both Shuto with palms facing outside, execute Jyodan-Haraiuke.
4: South

Point: Execute Moroteuke in squeezing elbows. Do not move ellbows up and down nor extend them wider than width of the shoulders. Same as in motion26.

足の動作●右足を軸に、体を左転して東に向け、左足をやや西に移して狭い四股立ちとなる。
立ち方●狭い四股立ち。
手の動作●両手刀のまま、右腕外側、左腕内側に交差し、両掌面を内向きに返し、両撓骨側上段払い受けをする。

着眼点●東

1: Pivoting on right foot, turn body to left facing east and bring left foot slightly toward west to become narrow Shikodachi.
2: Narrow Shikodachi
3: While both hands are remaining as Shuto, cross them with right arm outside, then, turn around them with palm facing inside. Execute Jyodan-Haraiuke with radius sides of both Shuto.
4: East

挙動の分解 13～15 Chinto Kumite in detail

⑫　⑬　⑭　⑮

▶チントウ篇　197

14挙動　　15挙動

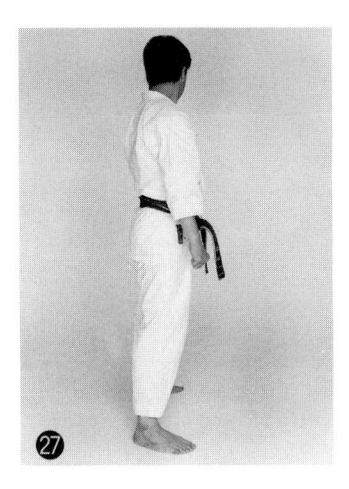

㉗　㉘　㉙

【㉘を東から見る】
㉘ seen from east.

足の動作●足はそのまま、両膝を伸ばして顔は北に向ける。
立ち方●狭い四股立ちの足幅。
手の動作●両手は握りながらおろす。

着眼点●北

足の動作●左足を北に進め、体を南に傾倒させる（左方からの上段突きを引き込み流す）。
立ち方●左足前の真半身後屈立ち（左膝を伸ばす）。
手の動作●左拳下段構え、右拳上段構えをする。

着眼点●北

1: Without changing foot position, stretch both knees and turn face toward north.
2: Standing narrow Shikodachi.
3: While clenching hands, pull them down.
4: North

1: Step left foot forward to north and lean body toward south (slip away from Jyodantsuki from left side).
2: Left-Kokutsudachi (stretch left knee).
3: Gedangamae with left fist and Jyodangamae with right fist.
4: North

チントウ

16挙動

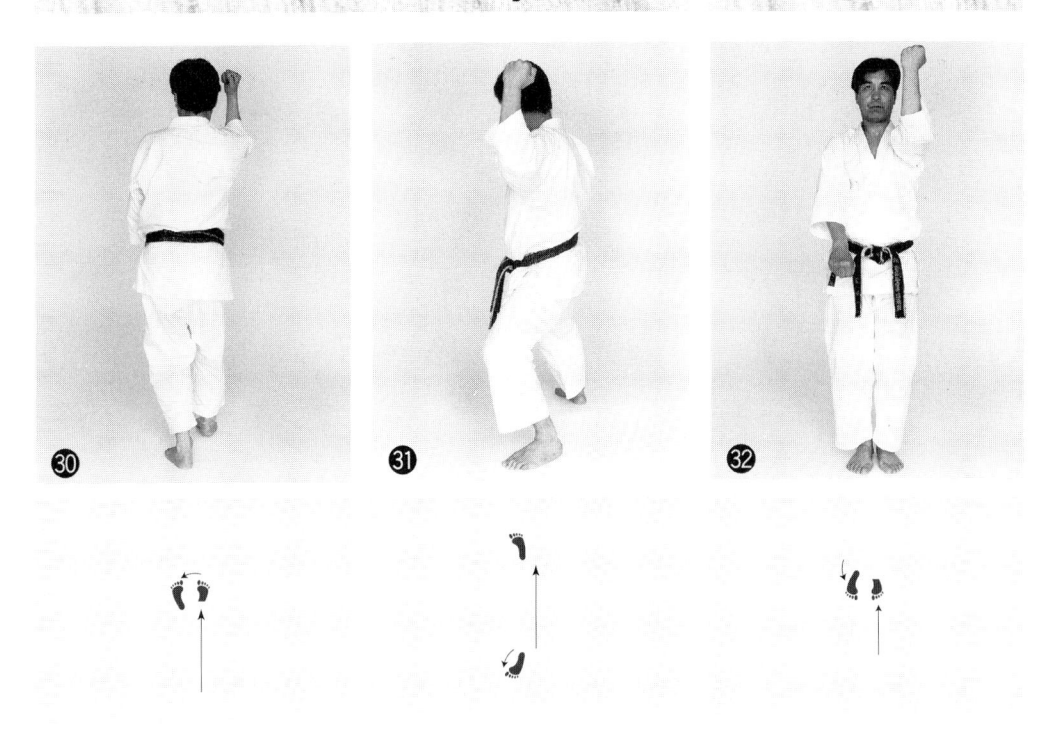

㉚

足の動作●左足を軸に、右足を左足に引きつけつつ、体をいったんまっすぐに起こしながら。
立ち方●左足に右足を引きつけ。
手の動作●（左右の構えは柔らかに）。

着眼点●北

1: While pulling ritht foot to left foot, raise body straight up at once.
2: Pull right foot to left foot together.
3: (Kamae with both hands must be supple)
4: North

㉛

足の動作●右足を北に進め、体を南に傾倒させる。
立ち方●右足前の真半身後屈立ち（右膝を伸ばす）。
手の動作●右拳下段構え、左拳上段構えをする。

着眼点●北

1: Step right foot forward to north and lean body toward south.
2: Right-Kokutsudachi (stretch right knee)
3: Gedangamae with right fist and Jyodangamae with left fist.
4: North

㉜

足の動作●右足を軸に、体を後ろ回りに（左に回転）しながら左足を引きつけ、いったん体をまっすぐに起こし、顔は一瞬南を向く（左右に相手を想定して動作する）。
立ち方●右足に左足を引きつけ（両足先はほぼ南を向く）。
手の動作●左右の構えは柔らかに。
留意点●一旦立ち上り、相手を意識しながら次の動作の方向に目線を向ける。北と南に相手を仮想し、南をふり向きながら南の相手を見つめ、次の瞬間、北からの上段攻撃を引き込み流す。

着眼点●南

1: Pivot on right foot. Pull left foot turning body back around to left, then, raise body straight up at once. Face to south briefly (as if preparing to move against opponent on left and right).
2: Pull left foot to right foot (toes pointing almost toward south).
3: (Kamae with both hands must be supple)
4: South

Point: While standing up, pay attention to next movement direction imaging opponents of south and north. Looking back toward south, look at eyes of opponent. Next moment, slip away from Jyodan attack of another opponent from north.

17挙動

㉝

足の動作●体を左転して左足を北に進め、体を南に傾倒させる（顔は北を向き、体は東向きとなる）。
立ち方●左足前の真半身後屈立ち（左膝を伸ばす）。
手の動作●左拳下段構え、右拳上段構えをする。

備考●13挙動の形に同じ。

着眼点●北

1:Turning body to left, step left foot forward to north and lean body toward south (facing north, but body faces east).
2:Left-Kokutsudachi (stretch left knee)
3:Gedangamae with left fist and Jyodangamae with right fist.
4:North

Note:Same as in motion 13.

18挙動

㉞

足の動作●左足の真後ろに、右足を爪先立ちにして運び。
立ち方●左足真後ろに、右足爪先立ちをする。
手の動作●両拳はいったん胸側に構えながら。

着眼点●東

1:Bring right foot just behind left foot standing on tips of toe.
2:Right foot on tips of toe just behind left foot.
3:Hold both fists on lower side of the body at once.
4:East

㉟

足の動作●足はそのままに、体を低く沈める。
立ち方●㉞のまま。
手の動作●左右同時に下段受け（左腕内側、右腕外側に交差）をする。

留意点●腰を曲げて下段受けをしないようにする。体の重心は両足の中心にとり、左足のみにかけないこと。

着眼点●東

1:Without changing position of feet, lower body further more.
2:Same as in 34.
3:Gedan-Uke with both fists at the same time (cross both arms with right arm on top).
4:East

Point:Dont't defend by Gedan-Uke with bending upper body. Weight should be put between both feet. Don't put weight only on left foot.

チントウ

19挙動　20挙動　21挙動

㊱　㊲　㊳　㊴

【㊳を東から見る】

㊳ seen from east.

足の動作●左足を軸に、右足を南に開き、狭い四股立ちとなる。
立ち方●狭い四股立ち。
手の動作●左右同時に撓骨側上段払い受けをする（両拳の掌側は内向き）。

着眼点●東

足の動作●その場で膝を伸ばして立つ。
立ち方●狭い四股立ちの膝を伸ばす。
手の動作●静かに両拳をおろす。

着眼点●東

足の動作●㊲のまま。
立ち方●㊲のまま。
手の動作●両拳を両腰にとり、両肘を外側に張って構える（両拳の甲は前方を向く）。

着眼点●東

1: Step right foot toward south to stand narrow Shikodachi.
2: Narrow Shikodachi
3: Execute Jyodan-Haraiuke with radius side of both fists at the same time (palms facing inside).
4: East

1: In the same position, raise body by stretching knees.
2: Extend knees of narrow Shikodachi.
3: Lower both fists slowly.
4: East

1: Same as in 37.
2: Standing naturally.
3: Hold both fists on waist and spread both elbows outside (back of hands facing forward).
4: East

22挙動 23挙動 24挙動

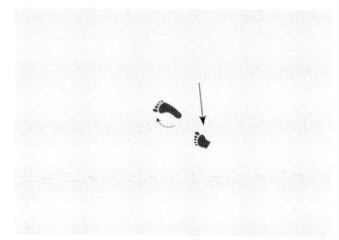

⓽ ㊶ ㊷

足の動作●その場で、体を落としながら、腰を左にひねる。
立ち方●狭い四股立ちの膝を軽く曲げる。
手の動作●前方からの中段突きに対し、右肘受けをする。左拳そのまま。
留意点●肘受けは腰の回転で行ない、それに伴って足先も変化する。手首を曲げたり、膝を固くして上半身のみを使って行なうのは受けが不充分となる。

着眼点●東

足の動作●その場で、体を右にひねる。
立ち方●㊵のまま。
手の動作●左中段肘受けをする。

着眼点●東

足の動作●右足を軸に、右回りして後ろを向き（西を向く）、左足を右足の真後ろ左脇に運ぶ。
立ち方●右足の真後ろ左脇に、左足爪先立ちになる。
手の動作●両拳の撓骨側で同時に上段払い受けをする。

備考●手の形は19挙動に同じ。

着眼点●西

1: In the same position, while lowering body, twist hips to left.
2: Bend knees of Narrow Shikodachi lighily.
3: Block Chudantsuki from front with right Hijiuke. Left fist remains the same.
4: East

Point: Hijiuke must be performed by hip turn, and then foot toe is moved. Executing with wrist only or upperbody only with stiff knee action will be an insuffiecient Uke.

1: In the same position, twist hips to right.
2: Narrtow Shikodachi
3: Left Chudan-Hijiuke
4: East

1: Pivoting on right foot turn to right with face backward. Then, bring left foot behind right foot on left side.
2: Stand on left foot of tips of toe behind right foot on left side.
3: Jyodan-Haraiuke at radius sides of both fists at the same time.
4: West

Note: Hands are same as in motion 19.

チントウ

㊸

㊹ 【㊸を西から見る】

㊸ seen from west.

㊺

㊻ 【㊺を西から見る】

㊸ seen from west.

足の動作●右足を軸とし、顔を左に向けると同時に、左足をあげて左足甲が右膝後ろに軽く触れるようにする（相手が左足を払ってくるのをかわす）。
立ち方●右片足で立つ。
手の動作●顔を左（南）に向けると同時に、左拳は左側方下段に払い、右拳は右側方上段に構える。

足の動作●㊸のまま。
立ち方●㊸のまま。
手の動作●右拳は胸側に引き、左前腕は胸前に横たえて、両拳を右胸側に構える（右拳下、左拳上に軽く触れ合う程度）。

着眼点●南

留意点●㊸──㊾連続動作。片足立ちとなり下段の構え（又は払い）と上段の構えが同時、中段の払いと蹴りを同時に行なうがこのときのリズムと引き拳、蹴りの引足が不充分な場合次の突きが弱くなる。一連の動作として評価する。

着眼点●南

Point:㊸-㊾Continuous movement.
While standing on one foot, Gedankamae (harai) and Jyodankamae must be executed simultaneously. However, insufficieut of the strength of rhythmical movement and Hikiken and Hikiashi in kick action will debilitate next Tsuki. These movements will be judged as a continuous movement.

1: Pivoting on right foot turn face toward left, lift left foot at the same time so that left instep touches back of right knee lightly (dodge opponent's side kick against left foot).
2: Stand on right foot.
3: While turning face toward left (south), hold left fist at Gedan on left side and right fist at Jyodan on right side.
4: South

1: Same as in ㊸
2: Stand on right foot.
3: Pull right arm to right side of the body and put left arm horizontally in front of chest, placing both fists on right chest (both fists touching lightly, with left fist on top).
4: South

▶チントウ篇 203

25挙動

【㊼を西から見る】

㊼ seen from west.

足の動作●左横蹴り（上足底）をなす。
立ち方●㊸のまま。
手の動作●相手の中段突きを左拳で横に払うと同時に、左横蹴りをする。右拳は引いたまま。

着眼点●南

1: Left-Yokogeri (with sole facing downward)
2: Stand on right foot.
3: While brushing sideways opponent's Chudantsuki with left fist, execute Left-Yokogeri. Right fist remains the same.
4: South

足の動作●左足を南におろし、右足を南に1歩進める。
立ち方●順突きの足（右前屈立ち）。
手の動作●右中段順突きをする。左拳は胸側に引く。

着眼点●南

1: Put down left foot toward south and take right foot one step toward south.
2: Right-Zenkutsudachi
3: Right-Chudan-Juntsuki. Pull back left fist to left side of body.
4: South

挙動の分解24、25　Chinto Kumite in detail

204

チントウ

足の動作●左足を軸とし、右足を引きあげる（前から右足を払ってくるのをかわす）。
立ち方●左片足で立つ。
手の動作●右側方に下段払い、左側方に上段構えをする。

備考●25挙動の㊿㊼㊷では、24挙動の㊸㊺㊼左右反対動作を行なう。

着眼点●南

足の動作●㊿のまま。
立ち方●㊿のまま。
手の動作●両拳を左胸側に構える（左拳下、右拳上）。

着眼点●南

足の動作●右横蹴り（上足底）をなす。
立ち方●㊿のまま。
手の動作●右中段横払いをすると同時に右横蹴りを行なう。左拳は引いたまま。

備考●㊿〜㊼は連続動作として評価する。

着眼点●南

1:Pivoting on left foot, lift right foot (dodge opponent's side kick from front against right foot).
2:Stand on left foot.
3:Gedanbarai on right side and Jyodangamae on left side.
4:South

Note: ㊿, ㊼ and ㊷ of motion 25 are reverse of ㊸, ㊺ and ㊼ of motion 24.

1:Same as in ㊿.
2:Stand on left foot.
3:Hold both fists on left chest (right fist on top).
4:South

1:Right-Yokogeri (with sole facing downward)
2:Stand on left foot.
3:While executing Right-Chudan-Yokobarai, execute Right-Yokogeri. Left fist remains the same.
4:South

52. Note: ㊿-㊼ will be judged as a continuous movement.

▶チントウ篇 205

26挙動

❺❸ ❺❹ ❺❺

足の動作●右足を南におろし、縦セイシャン立ちになる。
立ち方●右縦セイシャン立ち。
手の動作●左中段逆突きをする。右拳は胸側に引く。

留意点●腰を充分ひねって逆突きの縦セイシャン立ちとなる。

着眼点●南

足の動作●後ろから左足を払ってくるのを、左足を引きあげてかわす。
立ち方●右片足で立つ。
手の動作●後ろをふり向きざま、左側方下段払い、右側方上段構えをする。

着眼点●北

足の動作●❺❹のまま。
立ち方●❺❹のまま。
手の動作●両拳を右胸側に構える（右拳下、左拳上）。

着眼点●北

1:Put down right foot toward south to become Tate-Seishandachi.
2:Right-Tate-Seishandachi (wide stance)
3:Left-Chudan-Gyakutsuki. Pull back right fist to right side of body.
4:South

Point;Perform Tate-Seishandachi for Gyakutsuki by twising hips sufficiently.

1:Lift left foot to dodge opponent's side kick from behind.
2:Stand on right foot.
3:As soon as turning around, take Gedanbarai on left side and Jyodan-gamae on right side.
4:North

1:Same as in ❺❹.
2:Standing on right foot.
3:Hold both fists on right chest (left fist on top).
4:North

チントウ

27挙動

⁵⁶ ⁵⁷ ⁵⁸

足の動作●左横蹴り（上足底）
をする。
立ち方●❺❹のまま。
手の動作●左中段横払いをす
ると同時に、横蹴りをする。
右拳は引いたまま。

着眼点●北

足の動作●左足を北におろし、
縦セイシャン立ちになる。
立ち方●左縦セイシャン立ち。
手の動作●右中段逆突きをす
る。左拳は胸側に引く。

着眼点●北

足の動作●左足を軸に、体を
右転し、南に四股立ちとなる。
立ち方●四股立ち。
手の動作●南をふり向きざま、
右手を開き、尺骨側で右中段
懸け受け、右手首の尺骨側で
懸ける（手首を外屈させてつ
かむ）形にする。左拳は引い
たまま。

着眼点●南

1: Left Yokogeri (with sole facing downward)
2: Stand on right foot.
3: While executing Left-Chudan-Yokobarai, execute Left-Yokogeri. Right fist remains the same.
4: North

1: Put down left foot toward north to become Tate-Seishandachi.
2: Left-Tate-Seishandachi
3: Right-Chudan-Gyakutsuki. Pull back left fist to left side of body.
4: North

1: Pivoting on left foot, turn body to right to become Shikodachi toward south.
2: Shikodachi
3: As soon as turning toward south, open right hand and execute Chudan-Haraiuke with ulna side of Right-Shuto. Bend right wrist outside in order to grab opponent's arm. Left fist remains the same.
4: South

28挙動

⑤⑨

⑥⓪

【⑤⑨を東から見る】
⑤⑨ seen from east.

留意点●中段懸け受けの肘が体側外に出て斜めに受けないこと。⑤⑧は⑤⑨を極める途中の動作。

Point: At Chudan-Kakeuke, elbows must not come out of the body and defend diagonally. Motion of ⑤⑧ is in the process of performing ⑤⑨.

29挙動

⑥①

足の動作●左足を軸とし、腰を右ひねり、右足をわずかに右に開き、南に縦セイシャンの足になる。
立ち方●右縦セイシャン立ち。
手の動作●左肘を立てて、下から突きあげるように、中段に左縦肘当て（右掌面に当てる）をする。

留意点●肘当ては肩より高くならないで縦セイシャン立ちとなる。次に左腰に構える拳はスピーディに構える。

着眼点●南

1: Pivoting on left foot twist hips to right and step right foot slightly toward right to become Tate-Seishandachi toward south.
2: Right-Tate-Seishandachi
3: Hold left elbow up and attack toward Chudan with left elbow as if hitting upward (hitting against right palm).
4: South

Point:
Hijiate must be performed at Tate-Seishandachi so that Hijiate performance is not higher height than shoulder. Succeeding fist holding at left hip must be done quickly.

挙動の分解28、29
Chinto Kumite in detail

⑳ ㉑ ㉒

30挙動

(62)

足の動作●(61)のまま。
立ち方●(61)のまま。
手の動作●腰のひねりをすこしもどし、左手を手刀にし指先を下方に向けて左腰横に構え、その掌面に右拳を甲面下向きに軽く添える。

着眼点●南

1:Same as in (61).
2:Right-Tate-Seishandachi
3:Returning twisted hips a little, change left fist to Shuto and hold it on left hip with fingers pointing downward, while placing right fist on it lightly with back of hand facing downward.
4:South

(63)

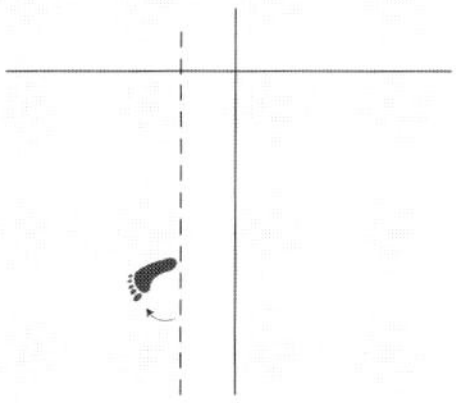

足の動作●後ろから左足を払ってくるのに対し、左足を引きあげてかわすと同時に前蹴りの構えをする。右足を軸とする。
立ち方●右片足で立つ。
手の動作●右裏拳で相手の鼻を掬いあげ打ち、左手刀は胸前に構える。
留意点●バランスを取ろうとして裏拳打ちを斜め横に打たないようにしなければならない。
着眼点●南

1:While lifting left foot to dodge opponent's kick from behind, take Maegerigamae.
2:Stand on right foot.
3:Sukuiageuchi to opponent's nose with right Uraken. Take a posture with left Shuto in front of chest.
4:South
Point:Do not execute Uraken-Uchi diagonally in order to keep balance of movement.

31挙動

(64)

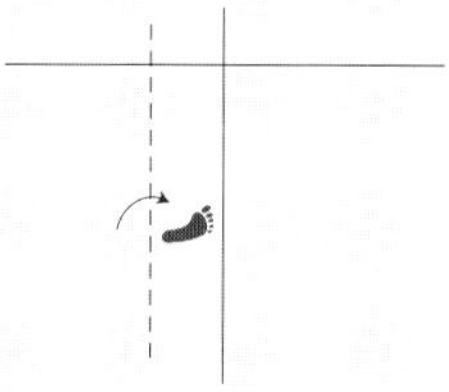

足の動作●右足を軸とし（右拳で掬いあげ打った調子に乗って）体を右に回転させ、後ろ（北）を向く。
立ち方●右に180゜回転し、右片足で立つ。
手の動作●体を右転し、北に向いて軽い左半身程度となり、両拳を右胸側に構える（右拳下、左拳上）。
留意点●中段横払いと蹴りは同時に行うが右の引手がゆるんではならない。
着眼点●北

1:Pivoting on right foot, turn body to right facing backward (toward north).
2:Turning right 180 degrees, stand on right foot.
3:Turning body to right, face toward north to become light left Hanmi with both fists onright chest side(with left fist top and right fist below).
4:North
Point:Chudan-Yokobarai and kick must be performed simultaneously and must not loosen right Hikite.

挙動の分解30、31　Chinto Kumite in detail

㉓

㉔

【⑥⑤を北から見る】
⑥⑤ seen from north.

【⑥⑦を北から見る】
⑥⑦ seen from north.

足の動作●左中段蹴り（上足底）をなす。
立ち方●⑥④のまま。
手の動作●左拳横払いと同時に左足で蹴りをする。右拳は胸側に引いたまま。

着眼点●北

足の動作●左足を北におろし、右足を北に1歩進める。
立ち方●順突きの足（右前屈立ち）。
手の動作●右中段順突きをする。左拳は胸側に引く。

着眼点●北

備考●⑥③～⑥⑦は連続動作として評価する。

1: Left-Chudangeri (with sole facing downward)
2: Stand on right foot. (Same as in ⑥④).
3: While executing Yokobarai with left fist, kick with left foot. Right fist remains the same.
4: North

1: Put down left foot toward north and take right foot one step toward north.
2: Right-Zenkutsudachi
3: Right-Chudan-Juntsuki. Pull back left fist to left side of body.
4: North

⑥③～⑥⑦ will be judged as continuous movement.

チントウ

止め

⑥⑨

直立

⑦⓪

足の動作●右足を軸に、体を左に回転させて後ろ（南）向きになり、左足を右足の東に引いて用意の姿勢にもどる。
立ち方●八字立ち。
手の動作●両手をそれぞれ大腿部前におろす。

留意点●止め、直立も、残心に留意する。

着眼点●南

足の動作●足を左、右ともどし、結び立ちに直る。
立ち方●結び立ち。
手の動作●両手は開いて軽く垂れる。

着眼点●南

1:Pivoting on right foot turn around body to left with face backward (south), then, pull left foot to east of right foot. Thus return to Yo-i posture.
2:Hachijidachi
3:Lower both hands in front of thighs.
4:South

Point:Pay attentions to Zanshin at Yame and Naore.

1:Pull left foot then right foot to return to Musubidachi.
2:Musubidachi
3:Open both hands and place them lightly on thighs.
4:South

▶チントウ篇 211

中央技術委員会　教範作成小委員会

蓮見　圭一　　　KEIICHI HASUMI
荒川　　通　　　TORU ARAKAWA
高島　　甫　　　HAJIMU TAKASHIMA
杉浦　健五　　　KENGO SUGIURA
塩見　　明　　　AKIRA SHIOMI
村田　　寛　　　HIROSHI MURATA
津山　捷泰　　　KATSUHIRO TSUYAMA
坂上　節明　　　SADAAKI SAKAGAMI

演武者
阿部　良樹　　　YOSHIKI ABE
橋口　優次　　　YUJI HASHIGUCHI
長谷川行光　　　YUKIMITSU HASEGAWA
前田　利明　　　TOSHIAKI MAEDA

演武補助
古川　哲也　　　TETSUYA HURUKAWA
影浦　健一　　　KENICHI KAGEURA
長谷川克英　　　KATSUHIDE HASEGAWA
野崎　　宏　　　HIROSHI NOZAKI

BB
BASEBALL MAGAZINE

新装版　空手道形教範

2001年7月2日　　第2版第1刷発行
2002年4月30日　　第2版第3刷発行

編　者　　㈶全日本空手道連盟

発行者　　池田哲雄

発行所　　㈱ベースボール・マガジン社
〒101-8381　東京都千代田区三崎町3-10-10
☎03-3238-0181（販売部）
　03-3238-0285（出版部）
振替口座　00180-6-46620番

Ⓒ Japan Karatedo Federation 2001　Printed in Japan　印刷・製本／共同印刷
ISBN4-583-03645-0　C2075

万一、落丁や乱丁がありましたらお取替えします。
定価はカバーに表示してあります。